Eyewitness
Spy

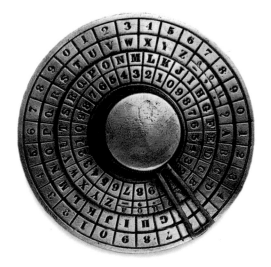

Night vision goggles

Hand-held transmitter

Laptop computer trace showing presence of bug in a building

James Bond's piton gun from *Goldeneye*

Side view of explosives pack for stay-behind agents in the event of World War III occurring

Ultraviolet lantern and anti-bugging seals

Prints made by SOE agent's rubber soles used to disguise beach landings

Ox tongue tin for
smuggling maps and
compasses, World War I

German invisible ink
and sponge

Eyewitness
Spy

Written by
RICHARD PLATT

Photographed by
Geoff Dann and Steve Gorton

SOE rubber soles worn
on boots to disguise
landings on beaches
and in deserts

Leather boot heel
with concealed
compartment,
World
War II

Message hidden
in rubber boot
heel, World
War II

Counter-
espionage
mirror for
looking
round
corners

Transmitter
for bugging
room

LONDON, NEW YORK,
MELBOURNE, MUNICH, AND DELHI

Project editor Miranda Smith
Art editor Kati Poynor
Assistant editor Julie Ferris
Managing editor Gillian Denton
Managing art editor Julia Harris
Production Charlotte Traill
Picture research Sarah Moule

Revised Edition
Consultant H Keith Melton
Editors Jayne Miller, Steve Setford
Art editors Edward Kinsey, Peter Radcliffe
Managing editor Camilla Hallinan
Managing art editor Owen Peyton Jones
Art director Martin Wilson
Associate publisher Andrew Macintyre
Production editor Laragh Kedwell
Production controllers Man Fai Lau, Pip Tinsley
Picture research Myriam Megharbi, Jo Walton

This Eyewitness ® Guide has been conceived by
Dorling Kindersley Limited and Editions Gallimard

First published in Great Britain in 1996
This revised edition published in 2009 by
Dorling Kindersley Limited, 80 Strand, London WC2R 0RL

Copyright © 1996, © 2009 Dorling Kindersley Limited
A Penguin Company

2 4 6 8 10 9 7 5 3 1
ED772 – 03/09

A CIP catalogue record for this book is available
from the British Library.

ISBN: 978-1-40533-780-9

Colour reproduction by Colourscan, Singapore
Printed by Toppan Co. (Shenzen) Ltd., China

Discover more at
www.dk.com

Silk map of
France used
by wartime
agent

Hand-held
transmitter
or "bug"

Doll made in Fresnes
prison by World War II
agent Odette Sansom

Matchbox created for Special
Operations Executive agent

Contents

Communications satellite
spying from the sky

What is a spy?

Rahab, who marked her windows with a red cord

SPYING, ALSO CALLED ESPIONAGE, began thousands of years ago, with nations battling for land, wealth, or slaves. Spies sneaked into the camps of their enemies, counting the number of warriors, or looking for plans of attack. If they were successful, they returned as heroes with the intelligence – the secrets – they had uncovered. Those who failed and were caught, faced execution. Throughout history, generals, governments, and business people have used words like CONFIDENTIAL and TOP SECRET to guard important data or documents. Spies are employed by such people to find out information that enemies would rather keep hidden, and pass secrets to people who were not originally intended to know them. Today spies still live dangerous lives. Some work like burglars to collect intelligence. Some have access to secrets because other people trust them. Spies most often reveal their secrets when enticed by money or to support another country's political system.

Joshua watches as the walls of Jericho tumble down

BIBLE ESPIONAGE
A story in the Old Testament, the holy book of Judaism and Christianity, tells how spies helped defeat the walled city of Jericho. The leader of the attacking army, Joshua, sent two spies into the town at dusk. They went to the house of a prostitute, Rahab, and hid on the roof. Rahab lied to the Jericho authorities to protect the spies, and when Joshua's troops destroyed the city, they spared the lives of Rahab and her family, but killed everybody else.

EGYPTIAN SPY
Ankhesenamen, young queen of Egypt, wanted to remarry when her husband Tutankhamun died in 1327 BCE. She wrote to a neighbouring king: "Send me one of your grown-up sons… he shall be king over Egypt." Instead, the king sent his assistant as a spy to check the queen's story.

SPYING FOR THE MONGOLS

Spies helped Genghis Khan (1162–1227) to conquer most of Asia. Khan came from Mongolia in central Asia, but he knew that people from Mongolia would soon arouse suspicion in distant lands. So he shrewdly recruited spies from among the target peoples, and these local spies were able to move around freely collecting intelligence. Over longer distances, he used horsemen who could ride ten times faster than an army could march to carry his secret messages.

Detail from 1459 map by Fra Mauro, showing Cathay, north China – part of Khan's empire

ALEXANDER THE GREAT

The Macedonian king Alexander the Great (356–323 BCE) used spies to find out about enemies' troop movements, and also to scout the best marching routes for his massive armies. Alexander's spies used a simple but effective technique to keep their messages secret. They wrote on narrow scrolls spiralling around a stick. Unwinding the scroll broke up the words of the message. But, wound around an identical stick, the text was easy to read.

The Bayeux Tapestry is actually embroidery on a linen strip 70 m (230 ft) long

Patterned bag hides camera lens

UNNOTICED IN THE CROWD

Some of the greatest spies of the past have been female: women could often go unnoticed where a man would arouse suspicion. In wartime, almost all young men joined the armed forces, and a man in civilian clothes was an unusual sight. In this photograph of Dutch spies at work during World War II (1939–1945), one of the women takes a picture with a hidden camera.

Daniel Craig as James Bond

RECORDED FOR POSTERITY

The Bayeux Tapestry shows spies in the historic Battle of Hastings in England in 1066. The tapestry records how an army from northwest France, led by William of Normandy (1028–1087), conquered England in 1066. English spies reported sighting thousands of clean-shaven men with short hair. At that time in England, all men except priests wore moustaches and long hair, so the spies assumed that they had seen thousands of French priests. In fact, these "priests" were soldiers who greatly outnumbered the English.

FICTIONAL SPIES

Dashing spy James Bond, agent 007, is the hero of 13 novels by English author Ian Lancaster Fleming (1908–1964), and more than 20 films based on them. Fleming was himself a spy before he began his career as a writer. He used the people he met during that time as models for the characters in his books. The plots of the books and the Bond films leave out the routine side of the lives of real spies. However, some of Fleming's own exploits were as daring as those of the fictional agent 007.

Types of spy

SPIES COME FROM many different backgrounds and either volunteer their services or are sought out and recruited by an espionage agency because they have access to secret information. Spies volunteering by walking into an embassy are called "walk-ins". Money is the most common tool used to attract spies in the world of espionage, but some are led by deeply-held beliefs. Others spy because they are being blackmailed, and still more because it makes them feel important. A plant is a spy who is working or serving in a target organization and this way can penetrate (work their way into) a position where they can collect intelligence.

TROUBADOURS
These medieval minstrels went from castle to castle entertaining European nobles. Some spied by listening to royal gossip and repeating the news when they travelled to another country.

Walker tramped Vienna's streets while Soviet agents checked that he was not being followed

Building (indicated by red arrow on map) mentioned in Walker's typed instructions for a 1978 visit to Vienna

CARELESS TALK
Spies do not make themselves obvious by wearing uniforms! This wartime poster warned British citizens that they should not gossip about sons and husbands in the armed forces because "Careless talk costs lives". Bus passengers listening to the conversation might be spies, and could report details of troop movements to the enemy.

INSIDER TRAPPED
French ambassador to Moscow Maurice Dejean unknowingly hired spies to work as his driver and maid. They used blackmail to try and turn him into an "agent in place". The plot failed, but Dejean's career was ruined.

WALK-IN WALKER
American John Walker worked for the US Navy and sold intelligence to the Soviet Union for 17 years. To meet them for payment and training, his Soviet handlers usually instructed Walker to travel to Vienna, Austria.

The splendidly-dressed Russian diplomats are "boyars" – members of noble Russian families

AMATEUR SPIES
Since Biblical times, traders have kept their eyes and ears open wide when they travelled abroad. These "amateur spies" are returning home from the land of Canaan to report what they had seen.

Iraq designed the "Supergun" to shell targets thousands of kilometres away

SPIES AND SUPERWEAPONS
Although the United Nations attempts to ban international sale of munitions to certain countries, intelligence services often work in secret to supply weapons to countries they consider their friends. In the 1980s a Canadian, Gerald Bull, received the support of Western intelligence services as he supplied Iraq with parts for weapons such as this "supergun" which was intended to be capable of striking both Iran and Israel. Bull was assassinated in 1990.

MOLE IN THE CIA
The nickname mole is given to serving intelligence officers who secretly work for another intelligence office – because they dig deep and work invisibly. Larry Wu Tai Chin, for example, was a CIA staff employee for more than 35 years and became a mole, spying for China.

SPIES AT COURT
Espionage is against the law in every country, and if caught spies face prosecution and punishment. However, throughout history, diplomats, such as the well-dressed figures in this 16th-century woodcut, have been in a good position to spy and they are protected. These civil servants represent their country in its embassies abroad, and they have a licence to spy. If they are caught, their diplomatic status protects them from punishment under international law. In fact, only very few work as spies. More are intelligence officers – they use their diplomatic jobs as a cover for recruiting and controlling agents who spy for them.

Procession of diplomats and merchants at the court of the Austrian archduke Maximilian II

9

Secret tool-kit

A spoof spy kit for the wartime spy

UNDERCOVER AGENTS OFTEN RELY ON AN ARRAY of sneaky tools, gadgets, and weapons. With these, a spy can bug a conversation or photograph a meeting. Other devices make escape easier, or hide the evidence of espionage from prying eyes. Fictional spy James Bond made gadgets famous. Before a dangerous mission, he visited the workshop of "Q" who supplied him with ingenious devices. The character is based on the inventor Charles Fraser Smith (1904–1992), who designed the equipment for the British intelligence services in World War II. Although Bond author Fleming was acquainted with Fraser Smith, Q was not in the original Bond books and was added only in the movies. Other organizations had equally inventive spy workshops – for example, Stanley Lovell (1890–1976) supplied the American OSS (Office of Strategic Services) with gadgets during World War II.

SUPER-SMALL SNAPPER
Spies must be able to take photographs without attracting attention. This tiny digital camera concealed inside a cigarette lighter case was carried in a spy's pocket to be available when an opportunity arose to take a secret picture. Such camera concealments are only effective in areas where smoking is accepted and would be discovered if the lighter was closely examined during a search.

Only slightly taller than a match

Lighter flips open to reveal camera

Pen writes normally

HANDY HEEL
Concealed items must be well hidden to escape discovery, and shoes and boots can hide quite large weapons or tools. In World War II, spies sometimes concealed gold, for bribery, and knives in their insoles. Hidden weapons also came in handy for those taken captive.

Strip is pulled to withdraw concealed item

Camera took four pictures when agent uncovered the pinholes

Exposures lasted minutes, so fixed objects such as buildings were the only practical subjects

Acoustic tube to microphone

PINHOLE CAMERA
Some of the tiniest spy cameras use pinholes instead of a lens. KGB agents used this one in the 1980s. The camera takes pictures that are not blurred, however close or far away the object. However, nothing is really sharp either!

LISTENING PEN
The circuits of radio transmitters are now so small that spies can install bugs in the tiniest of objects. This pen is inconspicuous in the pocket, and would not attract attention in a desk drawer. However, it conceals a microphone to eavesdrop on any nearby conversation. A tiny transmitter broadcasts the signal on UHF radio frequencies. The power of the signal is low, but strong enough for an accomplice who may be sitting in a car 500 m (1,640 ft) away to pick up the conversation with a receiver and record it.

Body of pen conceals transmitter

A BRUSH WITH THE ENEMY
All spies risk capture, but the danger is perhaps even greater in wartime. So World War II spies hid all kind of escape equipment in objects like this hairbrush. A compartment contains a saw to cut through prison bars, a map of enemy occupied territory, and a compass.

Pulling bristles lifts compartment "lid"

Tube houses battery with enough power for up to six hours

Miniature saw blade

Compass

Compass needle

Devices hidden in hairbrush

EASY ACCESS
The safest way to enter a locked building is to bribe a low-paid employee to unlock the door. Where this is not possible, spies may try to pick the lock with specially shaped tools like these. In Britain, intelligence services employed a retired burglar to teach this vital skill to wartime agents.

By inserting one of the hooked blades into a lock and turning gently, the tool lifts levers that hold the bolt in place

Map printed on thin paper to fold up small

Base of brush is hollow

Specially-shaped instruments are called picklocks

Range of picklocks enables agent to tackle locks of different sizes

Picks fold away into penknife-like handle

CHEATING AT CARDS
In World War II escape maps concealed in a pack of playing cards were smuggled into Prisoner of War camps to help plan escapes. Tearing each card apart revealed a small area of the map. The map fitted together like a jigsaw.

Seeing the invisible

VISUAL SURVEILLANCE is carried out by trained intelligence officers. They learn to use their eyes and cameras to collect intelligence, or for gathering information to blackmail their enemies. They use technology to make their vision keener. Magnifying lenses give a closer view of private scenes, while some night vision equipment makes photography possible even in a candle-lit bedroom. However, the clearest pictures do not guarantee the success of a surveillance mission. When spies secretly photographed a Western diplomat with his girlfriend, they were sure they could use the pictures for blackmail. They met the diplomat and threatened to send the pictures to his wife. His shameless response shocked them. "What wonderful shots!" he exclaimed. "Can you make me copies?"

NOSY NEIGHBOURS
The well-equipped spy does not need to stretch to get a better view.

ZOOMING IN
Sometimes spy agencies make use of commercially available equipment such as this high-resolution 35 mm camera with zoom lenses. The surveillance specialist photographs targets from long-distance either from a fixed observation post (OP) such as an apartment window or roof top, or a mobile OP (a car, or on foot). The purpose of a surveillance photo is to get intelligence information about a place, person, or activity (a clandestine meeting, exchange, or operation).

CAUGHT IN THE ACT
To photograph subjects in near darkness, surveillance photography is carried out with either infrared film and a concealed infrared light source, or night vision optics fitted to the camera (opposite) using ambient light (light that already surrounds the object). Infrared light usually produces better photographs of documents or other targets, but it also might be detected by an alert counterspy. Ambient light is completely "passive" and undetectable, but since it does not record colour, pictures have an eerie green glow.

Agent using a night-writing pen

Filters enhance image

Screen on back of camera allows user to check images taken before they leave the scene

Images are stored on a removable memory card inside the casing

An ordinary lens takes in the whole of the street market.

The powerful 300 mm lens picks out two particular figures from the crowd.

Two small batteries power goggles all night

Tubes make light 50,000 times brighter

Eyepieces adjust to suit the eyesight of individual spies

OH 1×20

SEEING IN THE DARK
Night vision goggles give spies the ability to see in very dim light. In total darkness an infrared torch casts a bright beam upon the scene for anyone wearing the goggles, but nothing can be seen by the target. Details differ, but most systems work like the image-forming tubes used on television cameras. The tube converts photons (packets of light) from the camera lens into electrons (tiny, electrically-charged particles). The electrons speed towards a phosphor screen, making a brilliant glow where they strike it. The screen forms a brighter copy of the original scene.

Twin lenses allow spy to judge distance

Lenses form life-size images so scene is not distorted and goggles can be used for night-driving

Strong harness supports heavy goggles

Side view of night goggles

Zoom lens functions as a telescope

ALL DONE WITH MIRRORS
Spies in 19th-century France used these innocent-looking binoculars to keep a watch on their opponents. One lens produced the same view as an ordinary pair of binoculars. The other was a dummy. Behind it, an angled mirror gave a perfect view of whatever was happening to one side – while the spy appeared to be staring straight ahead. A similar device is still available today. Disguised as a lens hood, it enables spies to photograph subjects at their side, while pointing the camera forwards.

Real lens

Focusing wheel

Dummy lens

Real lens inside

Hole for angled mirror

13

Bugs and taps

BEFORE YOU WHISPER "Tell me!" in a friend's ear, take a careful look around. Whispered words seem secret, but with bugs and wiretaps, spies can make sure that no conversation is really private. Like the insects they are named after, bugs are often tiny. They usually contain a microphone, power-source, transmitter, and antenna. A spy who tunes a radio receiver to the correct frequency can hear every sound that reaches the bug, even if he or she is elsewhere. Telephone bugs or transmitters perform the same service each time a telephone is used. Digital (and tape) recorders make it easy to monitor wiretaps and bugs. When there is a sound, recording starts automatically, and the device stops after there have been a few moments of quiet.

SENDING...
A basic bug or transmitter can be very small indeed. This one is the size of a matchbox.

...AND RECEIVING
This pocket-sized receiver picks up signals from the bug (left), relaying them to headphones or a tape recorder. The bug is a "quick plant" type, small enough to hide behind a picture. Its battery lasts a week. The bug is cheap enough to abandon – returning to collect it doubles the risk of discovery.

The 20-cm (8-in) bug found inside seal

EMBASSY SEAL
A gift from the Soviet Union, this replica eagle seal of the United States decorated that country's embassy in Moscow. In fact, the seal housed an ingenious bug. Sound made a spring inside the seal vibrate. Spies in a nearby building were able to detect the vibrations by using radar, and interpret the words that caused the vibrations.

CIA microphone wristwatch

WHAT IS THE TIME?
This CIA wristwatch conceals a microphone. It is normally inconspicuous, but in 1977, a US embassy official in Moscow created suspicions about his diplomatic intentions when he visited KGB headquarters wearing two watches.

Link to tape recorder hidden in agent's clothing

PHONE-TAPPING
Telephone taps can be easier to place than bugs because spies need not enter the room they want to listen to. Unless there is a switchboard, a telephone tap can go anywhere between the telephone and the exchange. In this film reconstruction from *Stakeout*, Chris Lecce (played by Richard Dreyfuss) uses a wiretap to keep a vital witness in an organized crime case under surveillance.

Flexible antenna broadcasts call to listening spy or recorder

Fibre-optic light-sensing device

Transmitter

Light-sensing device causes transmission to shut down when receiver is replaced

TELEPHONE TRANSMITTER

A telephone transmitter has the advantage that the "target" picks up the microphone and speaks directly and clearly into it! But the spy hears only the telephone calls, not any other speech in the room.

Crocodile clip connects to telephone line

Spy sets transmission frequency here

Wiretap is connected directly to line

WIRETAP

Sometimes a phone line can be tapped by connecting a couple of wires to leads in the junction box where the telephone line enters the building.

Telephone tap connected by clips to a chosen line

Bug powered by lithium is harder to detect than bug that draws power from telephone line

TELEPHONE BUG

In an office block where there are many extensions and a switchboard, a spy would need to install taps on every outside line and sift through many hours of tapes to hear just one short call. However, if a spy can enter the building unnoticed, a practical solution is possible – fitting a bug to a particular telephone. The spy can then either eavesdrop directly or record conversations and listen at leisure.

Microprocessor unit picks up signals from light-sensing device and activates transmitter

The microphone may be activated remotely by spy software

MOBILE BUGS

Modern mobile phones are software-based and make it easier to be bugged by a clever adversary who sends a message containing a malicious code. Once received, the code takes over and allows conversations to be digitally monitored and retransmitted along with copies of the user's emails and files to the eavesdropper's secret internet site.

A red dot reveals the user's position on the map

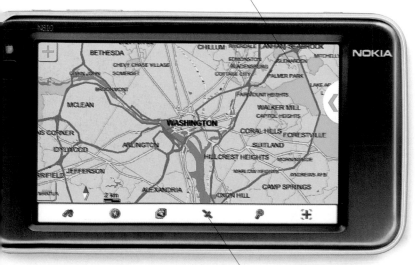

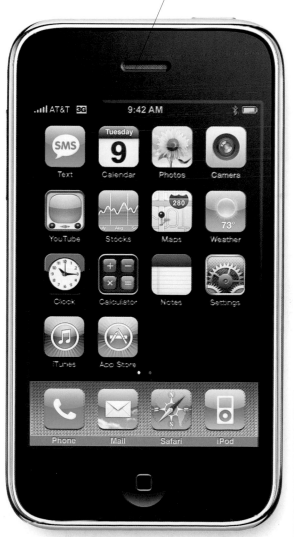

KEEPING IN TOUCH

Any time a mobile phone is turned on, its location can be pinpointed by the authorities and the user's movements tracked. Spies sometimes modify the software on mobile phones to allow them to secretly monitor the location and travel route of their surveillance target. Then they can listen in and follow their target through the phone.

The software for GPS satellite positioning is built into most new mobile phones

Listening in

Bugs do not always have a great range. The receiving distance is determined by the transmitting power, obstacles blocking the signal, and the level of radio interference from other radio users in the area. Lower power bugs are always desirable since the weaker signal is also harder for a counterintelligence service to detect and so locate the bug. The "listening post" – the receiving station – could be in an adjacent building, in a parked car, or even in the spy's pocket. The bug can be hidden in clothing if an agent has arranged a meeting with a contact in a street or park. Agents use cordless earphones and separate surveillance frequency to monitor and coordinate their activities surrounding the target area.

Pin-sized antenna

If the microphone built into the case is plugged into the phone, then a switched-on mobile phone resting inside a case can allow others to eavesdrop on or to record an encounter

Shirt hides induction loop, that picks up the conversation

Receiver can switch between two different bugs

BUG IN THE EAR

With wiring hidden under his shirt, an agent can monitor a bug without wearing conspicuous headphones. The listening device fits in the ear and looks like a hearing aid. The wire round the agent's neck creates an induction loop – a magnetic field that relays the amplified signal from a pocket receiver to the ear.

WEARING A WIRE

The radio signal from a bug hidden in a spy's clothing can alert counter-espionage agents operating bug detection equipment (pp. 48–49). A miniature recorder gets around the problem because it does not broadcast a radio signal.

Wearer uses remote switch on microphone to activate it to record anything interesting

A BETTER RECEPTION

Although some general-purpose receivers can pick up bug signals, specially-designed units are often more convenient and provide a better reception. This battery powered model links up with a portable recorder for unattended monitoring. An agent who set it up to receive signals from a telephone tap would need to return to the device only occasionally to change the tapes.

Telescopic antenna

Car battery can power receiver for extended operation

Socket for headphones

Lorraine Electronics
LONDON

UXR3

DIGITAL PEN

This pen is useful for more than taking notes – it is an unobtrusive way to record conversations and phone calls in an office, lift, or perhaps an informal chat over lunch. Many pens download voice files straight on to a PC.

Pen conceals a tiny digital recorder – some record for more than 12 hours and can be operated by remote control

STAKEOUT

Hidden microphones are legally used to investigate serious crimes and threats to national security. In the film *Stakeout* the head of security for a large American corporation listens in to a suspicious conversation. Laws limit the use of bugs, but some citizens' rights groups fear the controls are too weak.

Bug is only 4 mm (0.16 in) thick, and can hide behind a credit card, or nestle between pages of a diary

Compartments in spine of case conceal the power supply and transmitter electronics

A digital voice recorder can store up to 70 hours of converstaions that can be downloaded directly to a computer

Pen contains minute bug

MAKING A CASE FOR BUGGING

Monitoring a meeting is a common task for both political and industrial spies. Digital recordings of conversations can provide evidence of unfair competition, or help thwart a take-over by rivals. Bugging a briefcase is a discreet way to make a lasting record of "hush-hush" deals. Microphones built into a case can pick up speech on the far side of a room. It can be recorded or transmitted to a monitoring device outside. Touching the lock and a brass rivet head at the same time activates the device. Mobile phones can be used to record or monitor conversations (pp. 14–15), and a bugged pen will attract no attention and allow the microphone to be close to the talker.

Dropping in

Homing pigeons have played an important part in intelligence work since the earliest days of espionage. Carrying a precious cargo of vital secrets, a spy's airborne courier, the homing pigeon, can soar high over enemy territory. Roman general Julius Caesar (100–44 BCE) used them to send intelligence messages during his campaigns in what is now France. Ever since, spies have valued the pigeon's speed and its ability to return home in almost any weather. More than half a million pigeons carried messages in World War I. Some even worked as spies – reconnaissance pigeons carried tiny cameras aloft to photograph enemy fortifications. In World War II, spies who located the launch sites of German "flying bombs" used pigeons as carriers to send the information to the Allied forces who bombed the sites.

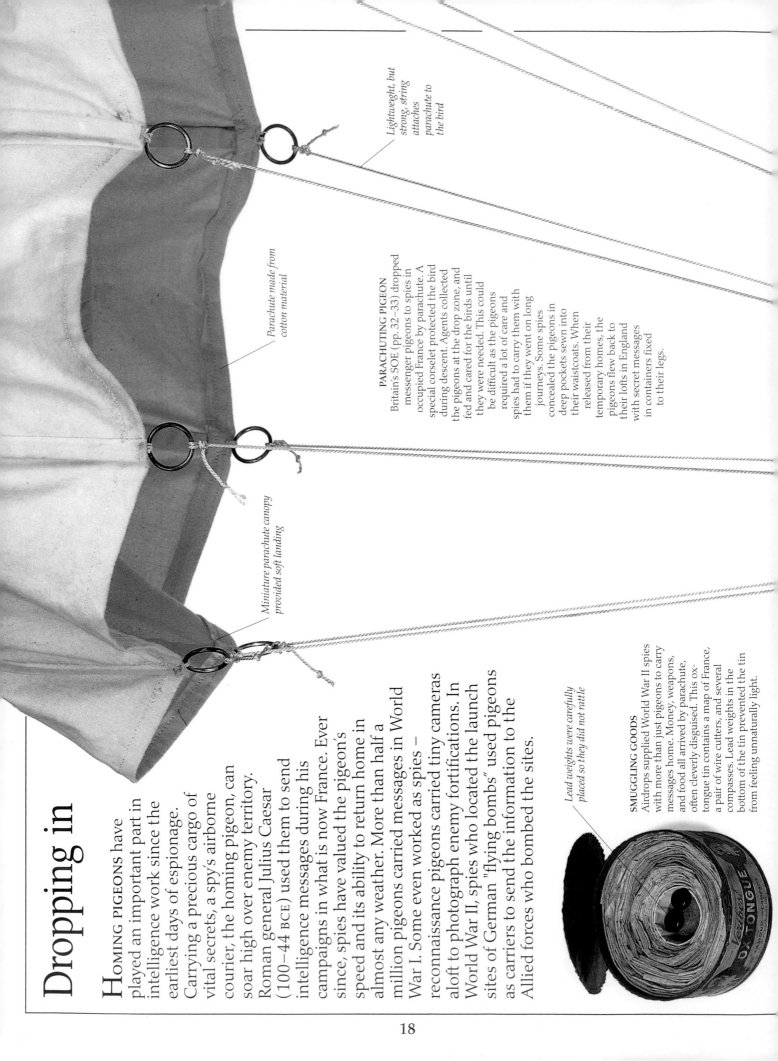

Lightweight, but strong, string attaches parachute to the bird

Parachute made from cotton material

Miniature parachute canopy provided soft landing

PARACHUTING PIGEON

Britain's SOE (pp. 32–33) dropped messenger pigeons to spies in occupied France by parachute. A special corselet protected the bird during descent. Agents collected the pigeons at the drop zone, and fed and cared for the birds until they were needed. This could be difficult as the pigeons required a lot of care and spies had to carry them with them if they went on long journeys. Some spies concealed the pigeons in deep pockets sewn into their waistcoats. When released from their temporary homes, the pigeons flew back to their lofts in England with secret messages in containers fixed to their legs.

Lead weights were carefully placed so they did not rattle

SMUGGLING GOODS

Airdrops supplied World War II spies with more than just pigeons to carry messages home. Money, weapons, and food all arrived by parachute, often cleverly disguised. This ox-tongue tin contains a map of France, a pair of wire cutters, and several compasses. Lead weights in the bottom of the tin prevented the tin from feeling unnaturally light.

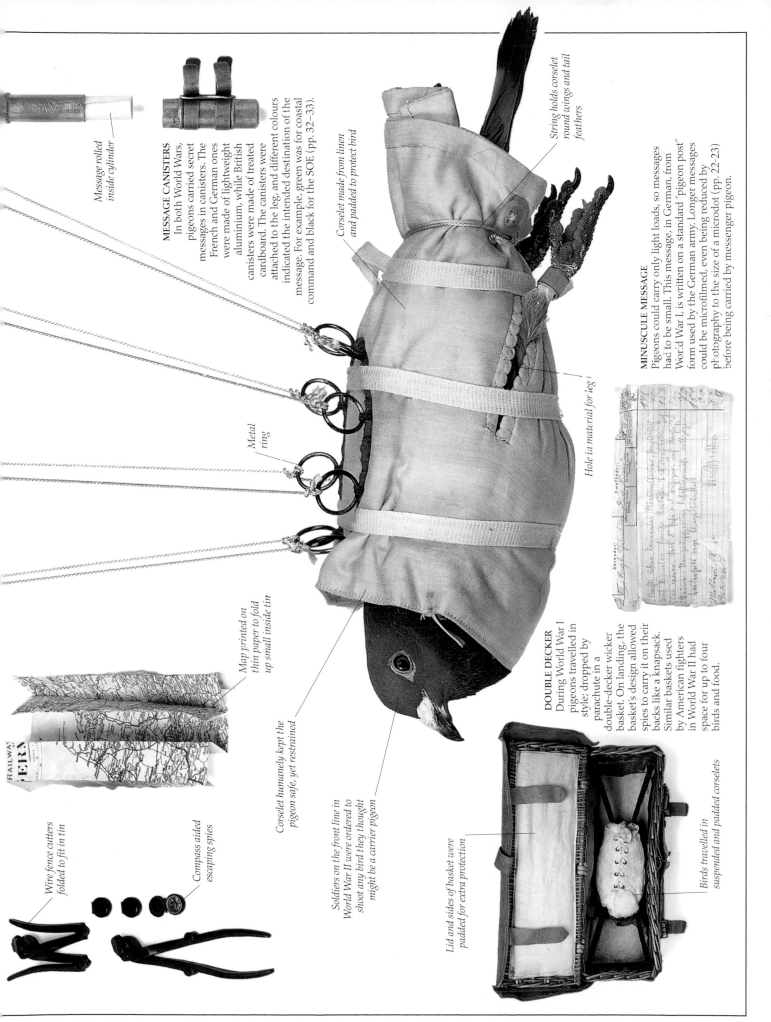

Message rolled inside cylinder

MESSAGE CANISTERS
In both World Wars, pigeons carried secret messages in canisters. The French and German ones were made of lightweight aluminium, while British canisters were made of treated cardboard. The canisters were attached to the leg, and different colours indicated the intended destination of the message. For example, green was for coastal command and black for the SOE (pp. 32–33).

String holds corselet round wings and tail feathers

Corselet made from linen and padded to protect bird

Hole in material for leg

Metal ring

Map printed on thin paper to fold up small inside tin

MINUSCULE MESSAGE
Pigeons could carry only light loads, so messages had to be small. This message, in German, from World War I, is written on a standard "pigeon post" form used by the German army. Longer messages could be microfilmed, even being reduced by photography to the size of a microdot (pp. 22–23) before being carried by messenger pigeon.

Corselet humanely kept the pigeon safe, yet restrained

Soldiers on the front line in World War II were ordered to shoot any bird they thought might be a carrier pigeon

DOUBLE DECKER
During World War I pigeons travelled in style; dropped by parachute in a double-decker wicker basket. On landing, the basket's design allowed spies to carry it on their backs like a knapsack. Similar baskets used by American fighters in World War II had space for up to four birds and food.

Wire fence cutters folded to fit in tin

Compass aided escaping spies

Lid and sides of basket were padded for extra protection

Birds travelled in suspended and padded corselets

Animal spies

IN THE PAST HUNDRED YEARS, military and intelligence services have sometimes trained animals to support and even replace the work of human agents or soldiers. Animals can make ideal spies, since they are rarely viewed with suspicion and tend to be overlooked because they blend in with the surroundings. Typically, they are trained to deliver secret messages or carry out reconnaissance missions, but sometimes they perform tasks beyond the capabilities of humans, such as laying bugging wires through drainpipes or tracking enemy agents by their scent. In the 1970s, the CIA experimented with robotic dragonflies, and today scientists are trying to use microchip-implants to turn live moths into miniature surveillance devices capable of being controlled remotely

SPIES WITH WINGS
During World War I, pigeons not only acted as secret message carriers (pp. 18–19) but also carried out aerial reconnaissance missions. The birds were trained to fly along specific routes and then released carrying tiny spring-driven motorized cameras, which took photos automatically at preset intervals. They returned with images of the terrain along the route, revealing the location of enemy forces.

MESSENGER DOGS
Pigeons were not only animals employed as messengers in World War I. Here, a German messenger dog leaps over a trench in 1917. Dogs could cover the ground two or three times faster than a person, and get through when it was too dark for signalling, or too foggy, wet, or dark for pigeons.

OPERATION ACOUSTIC KITTY
In 1961, the CIA surgically implanted electronic devices into a female cat to turn her into a mobile bugging device. The plan was to teach Acoustic Kitty, as she became known, to follow a specific route that would take her to within eavesdropping distance of an Asian head of state. The technology worked fine, but in training Kitty all too often wandered off the route. The project was abandoned, the devices removed, and Kitty lived out the rest of her life as a normal (non-spy) cat.

Microphone in ear canal

Wire antenna woven into fur

Transmitter and battery

ANTI-SUBMARINE SEAGULLS
In World War I, British admiral Sir Frederick Inglefield wanted to train seagulls to defecate on the periscopes of German U-boat submarines to "blind" them. Dummy periscopes were set up in Poole Harbour, Dorset, but the birds proved uncooperative. During World War II, the US Navy considered using seagulls to reveal the location of U-boats. By coating dummy periscopes with fish oil, it was thought that the birds might be trained to fly patrols off the US coast and land on the periscopes of submarines lurking offshore. The plan was never followed through.

CIA DEAD RAT DROPS
To pass secret communications to agents in Moscow, the CIA used dead rats that had been disembowelled to create a storage cavity in their stomachs. Money, film, and secret cipher material could be hidden in the cavity, and the rat left on a Moscow street for retrieval by an agent. When hungry cats began eating the rats before they could be recovered, the CIA doused the rats in hot-pepper sauce to deter them!

SCENT TRACKERS

In the Cold War, East Germany's Stasi trained male German Shepherd dogs to track hormone scents secreted by female dogs. The scents were placed on the doormats of suspected spies to contaminate their shoes. The dogs could then track the targets through the East Berlin streets for up to three days. Other methods used sterile cloths to capture a person's scent from their car seat or where they had been standing. Kept in an airtight jar, the scent samples stayed "fresh" and could be used for tracking years later.

Jar of scent samples from the Stasi museum in Berlin

RODENT AGENT

Officers from MI6, the British intelligence service, once used a mouse to help bug the apartment of a suspected Russian spy in Lisbon, Portugal. MI6 agents trained the mouse to carry a radio wire from a microphone in the loft through the bends in a drainpipe to a receiver in an apartment below the suspect's home.

DRAGONFLY IMPERSONATOR

The Insectothopter was a miniature UAV (Unmanned Aerial Vehicle) developed by the CIA's research and development office during the 1970s to eavesdrop on conversations. This robot bug was the size of a dragonfly, and was hand-painted to look like one. The four wings were powered by a tiny petrol engine. The Insectothopter was test-flown in 1976, but the project was abandoned when the Insectothopter was found to be too difficult to control in crosswinds.

Robot bug was designed to hover outside windows.

FINNED AGENTS

The US Navy uses specially trained dolphins and sea lions to patrol harbours in search of mines, enemy spies, and saboteurs who might be trying to plant explosives on the hulls of US ships. The dolphins can also be trained to photograph the secret design of a foreign ship's hull. There have been claims that the Navy has even tried equipping dolphins with poison-dart guns that could be fired underwater to stop enemy-agent divers, although the Navy denies this.

Sphinx moth

BIONIC MOTHS

US government scientists have experimented with implanting microcomputers into a sphinx moth in an attempt to control its movements and use the moth to collect and transmit data. Electronic sensors convert the moth's muscle vibrations into power for the on-board microcomputer. The plan is eventually to mount the bugs with surveillance equipment for use in reconnaissance missions too risky for human agents.

Secret messages

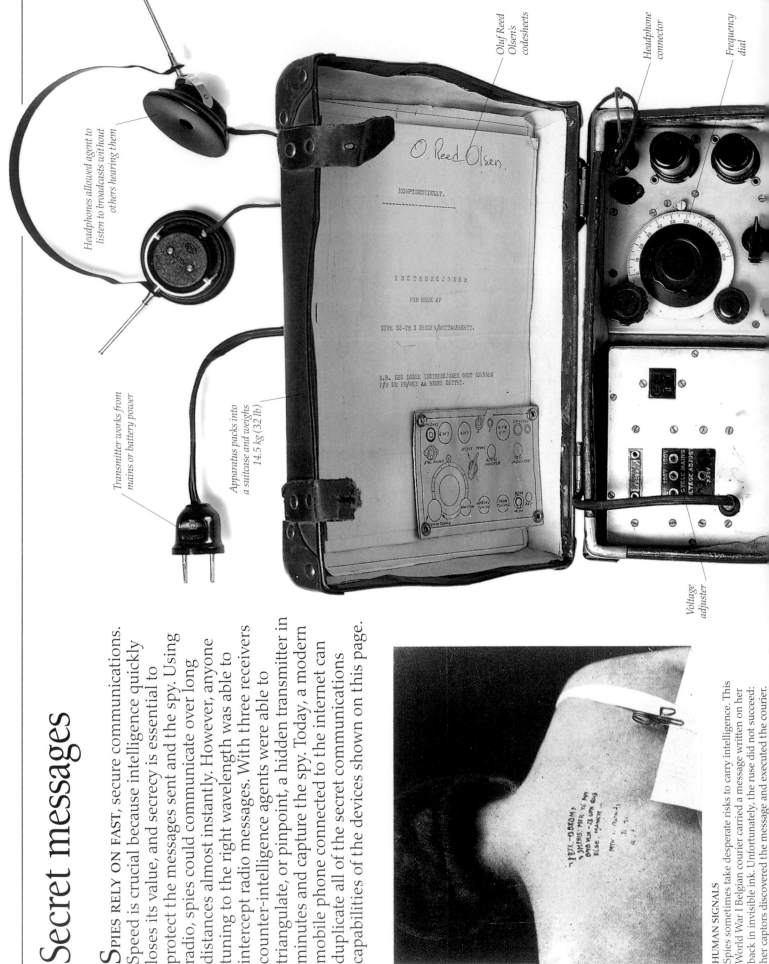

SPIES RELY ON FAST, secure communications. Speed is crucial because intelligence quickly loses its value, and secrecy is essential to protect the messages sent and the spy. Using radio, spies could communicate over long distances almost instantly. However, anyone tuning to the right wavelength was able to intercept radio messages. With three receivers counter-intelligence agents were able to triangulate, or pinpoint, a hidden transmitter in minutes and capture the spy. Today, a modern mobile phone connected to the internet can duplicate all of the secret communications capabilities of the devices shown on this page.

Headphones allowed agent to listen to broadcasts without others hearing them

Transmitter works from mains or battery power

Apparatus packs into a suitcase and weighs 14.5 kg (32 lb)

Oluf Reed Olsen's codesheets

Headphone connector

Frequency dial

Voltage adjuster

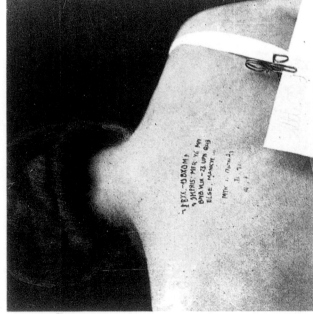

HUMAN SIGNALS
Spies sometimes take desperate risks to carry intelligence. This World War I Belgian courier carried a message written on her back in invisible ink. Unfortunately, the ruse did not succeed: her captors discovered the message and executed the courier.

Spare valve

Crystal plugs in to change transmission frequency

Antenna – an 18-m (60-ft) length of wire – plugs in here

Terminals attached to car battery for transmission without mains power

Spare tubes were carried in this compartment

Tapping key sends coded messages as long and short pulses of radio waves

NORWEGIAN SECRET AGENT

When German forces invaded neutral Norway in 1940, Oluf Reed Olsen fled the country in a sailing boat. Reaching Britain, he trained as a radio operator, returning to Norway in 1943, where spies in the Kristiansand naval base supplied him with details of German shipping movements. Olsen coded the messages and transmitted them to Britain from a camouflaged camp hidden in the trees above the harbour at Kristiansand. He used the radio set shown here. The cipher was considered unbreakable because it was based on sets of random numbers of which Reed Olsen and MI6 held the only copies.

Oluf Reed Olsen using the suitcase radio at his camouflaged base in 1944

Message can be reduced until it is the size of a full stop

MICRODOTS

Photography provides agents with a simple way to send messages secretly. By photographing a document with a special camera, a spy can produce a microdot – a negative that is 300 times smaller than the original. This paragraph about microdots can be reduced to a microdot the size of a full stop, and then hidden in a perfectly innocent letter. The agent who receives the microdot with the help of a microscope.

CONVICTED BY RADIO

Peter and Helen Kroger hid a radio transmitter under the kitchen floor of their bungalow. With it they transmitted British submarine secrets to Russia. They chose a house in west London, England, close to three busy airports, hoping that communications between aircraft and control towers would hide their secret signals. At their trial in 1961, the radio was used as evidence.

DOTTY PHOTOGRAPHY

Microdot cameras can be simple in construction, and small enough to hide easily. However, microphotography is difficult to do. Unless agents are very careful with the exposure of the film and its processing, the dot will be impossible to read.

Microdot camera (actual size)

MICRODOTS

Photography provides agents with a simple way to send messages secretly. By photographing a document with a special camera, a spy can produce a microdot – a negative that is 100 times smaller than the original. This paragraph about microdots can be reduced to a microdot the size of a full stop, and then hidden in a perfectly innocent letter. The agent who receives the letter can read every word of the microdot with the help of a microscope.

Codes and ciphers

ESPIONAGE AGENTS use "codes" and "ciphers" to communicate and keep their messages secret. In codes, letters, numbers, or symbols replace either the words or the entire meaning of a message or signal. Some codes are in general use. For example, when you post a letter, a postcode guides it to the right destination. Spies sometimes send messages in Morse code – dots and dashes that all radio operators understand. Other codes and ciphers are very complicated and difficult to break. Ciphers are a type of code but they have a secret "key" for encrypting the message – translating it into a cipher. The key can be a number, a word, even a poem. Anyone who has been given the key can easily decrypt the signal – change it back to plain text. Without knowing the key, the message reads as nonsense.

SIMPLE CIPHER
Ciphers do not need to be complicated if it is important only to hide their meaning from a casual glance. This jolly figure from World War I spells out "Ypres" (the site in Belgium of a famous battle) and a date, the "8th".

CIPHER DISC
This metal cipher disc, invented in 1802, is less than 6 cm (2.5 in) in diameter. The two inner circles are rotated to align with different letters and numbers on the outer two circles. This produces a simple, easily-broken substitution cipher in which each letter stands for another, so "W", for example, represents "E" whenever it occurs.

Code sheet is tiny so Yvonne Cormeau could easily hide it

CODE SHEETS
Charts like these convert a commonly used operational phrase into a coded word. It saves time and effort for the agent. These miniature code sheets were hidden in the handbag of SOE wireless operator Yvonne Cormeau in World War II (pp. 32–33). When she used a chart for Morse transmissions, a different letter would replace "E" each time it occurred in the message.

Baden-Powell drew sketches of insects before he set out so he could adapt them easily when in the field

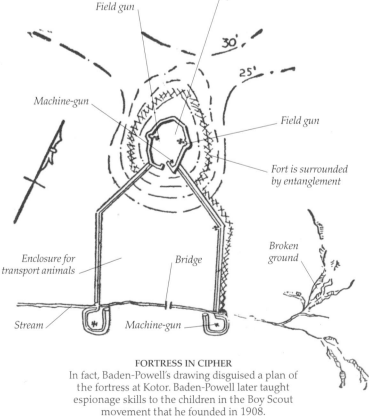

Moth's head conceals a fort on a knoll

Field gun

Machine-gun

Field gun

Fort is surrounded by entanglement

Enclosure for transport animals

Bridge

Broken ground

Stream

Machine-gun

BUTTERFLY SKETCHES
The eccentric English spy Robert Baden-Powell (1857–1941) disguised himself as a butterfly collector for one of his intelligence-gathering missions in Montenegro, on the coast of the Adriatic Sea. While he was there, he sketched this specimen of a moth perched on a twig.

FORTRESS IN CIPHER
In fact, Baden-Powell's drawing disguised a plan of the fortress at Kotor. Baden-Powell later taught espionage skills to the children in the Boy Scout movement that he founded in 1908.

Lid holds spare
light bulbs

Numbers between
the symbols
represented
people's names

Coded letter signed by
Anthony Babington,
conspirator in a plot to
assassinate Elizabeth I

ROYAL CIPHER

Mary Queen of Scots (1542–1587)
encrypted messages to allies outside her
prison walls (pp. 28–29). In the substitution
cipher that they used, the same symbol
stood for a letter each time it appeared,
so that the cipher was easy to break.

Bulbs lit behind
lettered windows
on the lid to indicate
enciphered character

Positions of rotors
controlled encryption
of each letter

Rotors spun after
each letter, ensuring
that cipher pattern
never repeated

Cipher was
keyed in

Connecting
sockets with
plugs made the
cipher more
complicated

SPEEDING UP ENCRYPTION

The Enigma cipher machine was used by
German soldiers (above), and diplomats to
aid intelligence in the 1930s and during World
War II. The signals baffled enemy cryptanalysts
(cipher experts) who intercepted them and
tried to break the cipher. The Polish secret
service, with the help of a recruited spy in
the German cipher office, was able to
interpret three-quarters of the Enigma
messages by 1938, and in 1939 passed
on this knowledge to Britain and France.

Rotors and
plugs gave
several million
million
combinations

Klappe
schließen

ENIGMA IN OPERATION

After setting plugs and three or four rotors, encryption on
Enigma was automatic. Pressing a letter key lit up a different
letter on the display above. The encrypted letter was different
each time. Decryption on the receiving Enigma machine
reversed the process. In principle, coded messages from the
Enigma machine were impossible to read without knowing
the rotor and plug settings. But that information and an
actual Enigma machine supplied by the Polish Secret Service
helped the British break most of the Enigma codes in an
operation called "Ultra" which remained secret until 1972.

Intercepts and code-breaking

CIPHER CLERKS AT WORK
Britain's code-breaking centre in World War II was at Bletchley Park near London, set up in August 1939. More than 5,000 staff worked on up to 2,000 encrypted messages a day.

CIPHERS HELP PROTECT secret messages, but they do not destroy the meaning completely. Like a word puzzle, the sense of the message remains locked inside. An enemy who intercepts the signal will try hard to find the key. Intelligence agencies employ code-breakers called cryptanalysts to do this. With a substitution cipher (pp. 24–25), a cryptanalyst starts by counting letters. In English, "E" is used more often than other letters. So, if in the message "W" appears most, it probably stands for "E". The next step is to look for two-letter words ending in "E". There are only four in English: he, me, be, and we.

Then the cryptanalyst will look for letters that stand on their own – in English there are just two one-letter words, "A" and "I". With techniques like these and even more complex ones, cryptanalysts can solve elaborate cipher puzzles, although it can sometimes take them a long time. Computers speed the process, but cryptanalysts need to be very patient. Few though, are as patient as a 17th-century Arab who deciphered a message to the Sultan of Morocco. It took him 16 years.

ZIMMERMANN TELEGRAM
Deciphered in Britain in 1916, this telegram was sent by the Germans to their ambassador in Mexico. It suggested that Mexico form an alliance with Germany and invade three southern US states. The interception of the telegram was possibly the most important spying event of the war. Shocked Americans quickly entered World War I on Britain's side.

"Bombe", named by Polish inventors after the ice-cream bombe they were eating at the time

WRENS (members of the Women's Royal Navy) operated the machines

GOING LIKE A BOMBE
Cryptanalysts at the code-breaking centre at Bletchley Park used some of the first computers to help them break codes and ciphers. In two hours a "bombe" could try every combination of rotor positions that was in use on the Enigma machines that Germany was using. When the bombe broke a cipher, it simply stopped. A later machine, called Colossus, was the world's first electronic computer, a forerunner of the laptops in use today.

Japanese aircraft bomb Pearl Harbor, 7 December, 1941

USS West Virginia *ablaze after suffering two aerial bombs and seven torpedo hits*

THE PURPLE MACHINE
Like Enigma (pp. 24–25), the Japanese Purple cipher machine used a plug board to create a huge number of possible keys. However, Purple used telephone switches in place of the rotors found in Enigma. A team of US cryptanalysts, including William Friedman (below left), cracked the Purple cipher by building a replica of the mechanism.

PEARL HARBOR PREDICTIONS
By cracking the Purple code (right), American cipher experts predicted a Japanese attack on 7 December 1941, but could not name the hour or the place. The spy Dusko Popov (pp. 56–57) had a microdot that contained intelligence questions about Pearl Harbor and Richard Sorge (pp. 34–35) had predicted that Japan would attack southwards. The intelligence wasn't enough – the devastating surprise raid took place on Pearl Harbor in Hawaii at 6:00am, when many US servicemen were still asleep. The attack killed 2,300 Americans, as well as crippling the American fleet, and drawing the United States into World War II.

HUSBAND AND WIFE TEAM
Russian-born American William F. Friedman (1891–1969) led the US Army Signals Intelligence Service team that cracked Japan's Purple cipher. Friedman worked on ciphers during both world wars. In the 1920s, his wife Elizebeth broke the codes of rum smugglers during prohibition, when alcohol was banned in the United States.

AMERICAN COMMISSION TO NEGOTIATE PEACE

PASS No. 92

Permit Bearer YARDLEY, H.O., Capt.

To enter HOTEL CRILLON,

PLACE DE LA CONCORDE

Signature of Bearer

R. H. VAN DEMAN
Colonel, General Staff
U.S.A.

PIONEERING CRYPTANALYST
Herbert Osborne Yardley (1889–1958) was a brilliant cryptanalyst and pioneered code-breaking for the United States during World War I and afterwards. He set up the US unit that became known as the "Black Chamber" to read foreign intelligence material. His work in the 1920s was later used to help break the Purple cipher.

Herbert Yardley's security pass

THE "DEAD SOLDIER"
In 1943, the drowned body of a British major was washed ashore in Spain. Papers he was carrying described plans by the Allies to attack Greece and Sardinia, and German troops immediately moved there. In fact "Major Martin" was actually a civilian who had died of pneumonia. Intelligence chiefs had arranged for his body to be dressed as a soldier, and pushed from a submarine off the Spanish coast. The Germans were completely taken in, and when they moved their troops, they left very few soldiers on Sicily – the Allies' real target.

Planted theatre ticket stubs made the major's story appear genuine

"Major Martin's" fake identity card planted by intelligence officers

NAVAL IDENTITY CARD No. 148228

Surname MARTIN

Other Names WILLIAM

Rank (at time of issue) CAPTAIN, R.M. (ACTING MAJOR)

Ship (at time of issue) H.Q. COMBINED OPERATIONS

Place of Birth CARDIFF

Year of Birth 190

Issued by

at ADMIRALTY

Date 2nd February 1943.

Photograph of living person who looked like "Major Martin"

Concealment

SPY RING
Microdots (pp. 22–23) reduce documents to the size of a full stop. In World War II, British agents hid them in this hollow ring.

A CLOAK AND DAGGER are the traditional trademarks of the secret agent. The spy hides the dagger, the badge of the assassin, under the cloak, which stands for secrecy, disguise, and concealment. Spies of the past could put on a cloak quickly to hide their true identity. Some chose more exotic disguises – Louis XV's agent the Chevalier d'Eon dressed as a woman for many years. For a modern spy, disguise is just as necessary, but much more subtle. Today's agents try to look ordinary, aiming to pass unnoticed in a crowd. Agents also choose ordinary-looking objects as hiding-places. Hidden in a working battery, a secret message is safe from even a close inspection. By miniaturizing their messages, spies can conceal them in even smaller objects. Large objects are more difficult to hide. But an ingenious and determined spy can hide heavy equipment, tank engines – even kidnapped people.

Wrist strap

Right-angle viewfinder

Lens

Direct vision viewfinder

Setting for bright light

Aperture setting knob

ROYAL BEER BARREL
Imprisoned by England's Queen Elizabeth I, Mary, Queen of Scots (1542–1587) smuggled messages to sympathizers in a beer barrel. She wrapped encrypted documents in a waterproof bag, probably an animal bladder. Then she pushed the bag through the bung hole into the barrel. Replies travelled back into her prison by the same route. Her "postman", a double agent called Gilbert Gifford, betrayed the scheme (p. 41).

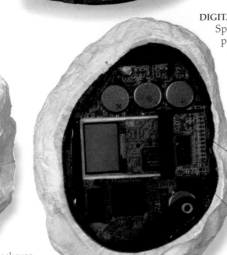

Wooden bung seals barrel when full of beer

Mary, Queen of Scots

SMILE PLEASE!
"Detective" cameras disguised as books, hats and neck-ties first appeared in the 1880s. As early as 1893 spies were taking pictures with cameras shaped like pocket watches. This wrist-watch camera dates from 1948. On its 25-mm (1-inch) diameter disc of film it takes eight pictures, each the size of a fingernail.

Cell provides 1.5 volt power

Compartment is big enough to hold a roll of film

Magnet grips base to unscrew it

BATTERIES INCLUDED
This ingenious hiding-place looks like a normal battery, and a cell inside provides enough power to light a bulb. However, there is a secret compartment at the base.

DIGITAL ROCK SPY
Spies leave messages in prearranged hiding-places, or "dead drops". Leaving a message at a dead drop is safer than arranging to meet an agent in person. British Intelligence used this digital dead drop inside a fake rock to receive, store, and retransmit messages to an agent in Moscow. Other digital dead drops can be created over the internet from anywhere in the world.

The fake rock was hidden by a busy road

Three round flat batteries provided power for the electronic circuitry

Small integrated circuits communicated secretly with the agent's mobile phone

Dukes as Comrade Piotrovsky

Dukes as an ailing intellectual

Dukes as a bearded worker

Dukes as a sufferer from epilepsy

Contemporary print of the Chevalier d'Eon

D'Eon complained that he sometimes forgot whether he was wearing a woman's headdress or a man's helmet

A SHADY LADY
The Chevalier d'Eon (1728–1810) was an expert fencer and lawyer. He began his career as a spy for French king Louis XV in 1756. He posed as a shy woman in the Russian court to gain the confidence of the Russian empress, and also worked as a double agent for the British. He lived in London as a female at the end of his life, and when he died, many people were shocked to learn his real identity.

AGENT ST 25
Paul Dukes became an expert in disguise as head of British intelligence in Russia. He was in Moscow in 1917 when revolution swept the communists to power. Pursued by the Cheka (secret police), Dukes cheekily posed as Comrade Piotrovsky, a Cheka officer. To the British, he was "Agent ST 25".

HOW TO SMUGGLE A SPY
In 1964, drugged and bundled in a trunk, Israeli Mordecai Louk narrowly escaped being exported from Rome to Cairo disguised as diplomatic mail. He was freed when a customs guard heard the box whimper. Louk had been spying in Italy for the Egyptians.

Clamps held ankles and neck

Small seat

Leather slots for feet

Trunk was only 137 cm (53 in) long

Spies at war

Advancing armies rely on expert soldiers to survey the land ahead, and judge the enemy's strength. However, not all are spies. Some are scouts who work openly and wear army uniforms. If they are caught, they spend the rest of the war in prison. Wartime spies, though, disguise themselves to avoid capture, and they collect information secretly. So anyone caught in enemy territory wearing the clothes of a civilian can be tried as a spy, and the punishment – usually execution – is immediate. Despite this harsh penalty, spies have operated in almost every war. The 18th-century German king, Frederick the Great, even bragged about the number he employed. Mocking a French commander as a gourmet, he joked "A hundred cooks follow him – but ahead of me go a hundred spies!"

Major Coleridge's diary, 13 July 1899

SOUTHERN BELLE
Many women worked as spies in the US Civil War (1861–1865) and Belle Boyd (1844–1900) became one of the most famous Confederate (Southern) agents. She learned military secrets from Union (Northern) officers lodged in her Virginia home, and braved gunfire to tell Confederate leaders. After capture and then release in a prisoner exchange, she received a heroine's welcome in the South.

DEATH OF A SPY
Major John André (1751–1780) was hanged as a spy during the American Revolution (1775–1783). He had gone to meet US traitor Benedict Arnold (1741–1801), the commander of West Point, a fortress which guarded the Hudson River Valley. Arnold wanted to surrender the fort to the British, and he handed André details of his plans. The ship that was to take André and the secret plans back to the British Army was fired on and left without him. André disguised himself as a civilian, but was caught by the American militia with the secret papers hidden in his boots. The British spy was hanged in 1780.

DETECTIVE SPYMASTER
When civil war divided the United States, Abraham Lincoln turned to a private detective to help gather intelligence for the Union army. The choice seemed to be a natural one – the Scotsman Allan Pinkerton (1819–1884), head of the famous detective agency, had already foiled one attempt to assassinate President Lincoln. Unfortunately, Pinkerton knew very little about war, and his agents were often clumsy and sometimes cowardly. He resigned as Lincoln's spymaster in 1862.

Hollow bullet used by Major Coleridge to hide his messages

FIGHTING THE BOERS

In the Boer War (1899–1902) British forces fought to control farms and gold in what is now South Africa. Their enemies the Afrikaners, or Boers, were descendants of white Dutch settlers. Major H F Coleridge was among those who spied for the British, and his diaries (left) record details of the Boer defences. The British intelligence service did not realize the value of the intelligence that spies like Coleridge supplied, and he had to plead for more money to continue his work (below).

CARTOON CAPTURE

During World War I (1914–1918), spies usually operated far from the front line, in neutral nations such as Switzerland and the Netherlands (Holland). Nevertheless, the public fear of spies and their exploits inspired many cartoons. This colourful example shows a German spy captured by French troops.

Coleridge sent this telegram asking for more money in 1900

French-born Violette Szabo was the best shot in Britain's SOE

COURAGEOUS COMMANDO

Violette Szabo was fluent in French and a skilful rifle shooter – London shooting galleries banned her because she always hit the target – perfect qualifications for a spy. She was approached by the SOE (Special Operations Executive) during World War II (1939–1945) and agreed, to avenge the death of her husband Etienne (above), who died fighting for the British in north Africa. She was admired by fellow spies for her courage and determination. She was captured after a gun battle on her second SOE mission in France, when she was sabotaging telegraph lines. Violette Szabo was executed in a German prison camp.

Lincoln (centre) dismissed his general (left) after the disaster at Antietam

On 17 September 1862, 12,000 Union troops died at the battle of Antietam, largely due to bad intelligence, and Pinkerton (right) resigned

TOO GOOD TO BE TRUE

The cleverest agent of World War II, codenamed "Cicero", was extremely good at spying for Germany. He was an Albanian and his real name was Elyesa Bazna. While working as valet to the British ambassador in Turkey, he opened the embassy safe, and photographed secret codes, lists of British spies, and the Allied plans to invade Europe. But these documents were so secret that the German leaders could not believe they were genuine, and ignored Cicero. Nevertheless, they paid him a fortune in banknotes – but all of them were forgeries.

A cover story

BITTER PILL
Some SOE agents carried a suicide L-pill (lethal pill) which would kill in seconds. No agent ever used it.

Disguised as a child's nurse, "Annette" passes through a wartime roadblock in southwest France. "Annette", who is really the radio operator Yvonne Cormeau, tells her cover story well, escaping capture for a year, and transmitting over 400 coded messages. During World War II, the lives of many secret agents depended on their cover stories – invented pasts designed to hide their real identity. In Britain, the Special Operations Executive (SOE) trained agents, giving them cover stories that they learned by heart. Then the SOE dropped the agents in France by parachute or small boat.

Fake French matchbox

POCKET KNIFE
Male and female agents carried pocket knives to help with sabotage if necessary, such as slicing through an enemy's car tyres.

VITAL TIMING
A late arrival usually signalled danger. Cautious agents did not wait more than a few minutes at a rendezvous.

PARTING GIFT
SOE agents were given a valuable present such as this silver cigarette case before leaving on a mission. The gift could be used as a bribe if an agent was caught by a corrupt official.

Wallet

Powder compact

MINI-MAPS
War agents used maps to plan sabotage. A silk map (above) folds very small to aid concealment.

TINY TAPPER
A Morse code key was small enough to hide easily in a handbag.

Mirror

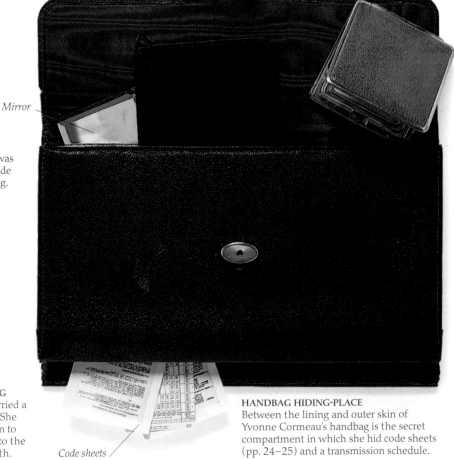

PLUG-IN TUNING
Yvonne Cormeau carried a variety of crystals. She could change them to tune her SOE radio to the correct wavelength.

Code sheets

HANDBAG HIDING-PLACE
Between the lining and outer skin of Yvonne Cormeau's handbag is the secret compartment in which she hid code sheets (pp. 24–25) and a transmission schedule.

The clothes had to be tailored in the French style of the 1940s

SOE carefully removed all English labels before sending an agent into enemy territory

Every detail of clothing reinforced the cover story – an agent posing as a clerk would wear a simple, inexpensive hat like this one

Yvonne Cormeau's tattered leather briefcase

Briefcase fitted in with one of Yvonne Cormeau's disguises – a district nurse

YVONNE CORMEAU, SOE RADIO OPERATOR

Many of these items belonged to Yvonne Cormeau, the SOE agent whose cover name was "Annette". She parachuted in to France on the night of 22–23 August 1943, and worked as a radio operator. Her natural caution helped her to avoid being captured until Allied forces liberated France in 1944. On one occasion, she recognized another agent on a train but resisted the temptation to speak – she had learned in training that if he was under suspicion, they might both be captured. On the other hand, Yvonne Cormeau knew when it was worth taking a risk. Although most radio operators moved their radio sets daily to avoid capture, she felt safe transmitting from the same house for six months. From the windows she could spot interception vans over 5 km (3 miles) away.

Stockings could be used as a bribe by the SOE agent as silk was very rare in wartime

Suede shoes

Agents, moles, and defectors

TRIBUTE TO A SPY
Richard Sorge (1895–1944) appeared to be a fanatical Nazi during World War II. While a political adviser to the German ambassador, he was feeding secrets to Germany's Russian enemies. Soviet stamps showed Sorge as a hero.

DOUBLE AGENTS ARE REALLY "controlled enemy agents". Rather than serving two masters they work for only one side in a war of espionage – but they deceive the other side into thinking they are working for them and instead steal their secrets. Being a double agent is very risky. To be successful they must develop the trust of an intelligence agency, while their sole aim is to betray that trust. If caught they can expect no mercy in their punishment. Double agents may be volunteers, or they could be spies unmasked by counter-intelligence agencies who have been "turned" (recruited and controlled) rather than prosecuted. Their new masters provide them with false but believable information, and the spy passes on the bogus secrets as if they were true.

Defectors are intelligence officers who leave their home country to go to another country and reveal the secrets brought with them. Although they may be admired in the country to which they are truly loyal, they earn hatred in the country they betrayed.

A TRAITOR'S DEATH
Japanese counter-intelligence agents unmasked Richard Sorge for their German allies. He was condemned in 1941 and executed in 1944.

Aldrich and Rosario Ames after their separate trials for spying

ANCIENT SPYMASTER
Chinese commander Sun Tzu was among the first to write about double agents. He called them "doomed spies" – who do certain things openly for purposes of deception and allow our spies to report them to the enemy. Sun Tzu wrote his book, *The Art of War*, in the 4th century BCE.

RUSSIAN AGENT AT THE CIA
For nine years Aldrich Ames (born 1941) was a Soviet spy while working as a trusted officer at the CIA. Ames and his wife Rosario provided details of many spies recruited by the CIA and, with their help, Moscow was able to build a network of double agents who deceived their CIA bosses. The pair were paid well by the Russians for their treachery.

«Если бы мне предстояло начать жизнь сызнова, я начал бы так, как начал».

Феликс ДЗЕРЖИНСКИЙ.

ДЕКАБРЬСКОЕ морозное утро, ночная мгла еще не ушла с заснеженных улиц. Деревья на Гоголевском бульваре покрыты пушистым инеем. У троллейбусной остановки — цепочка по-

представить все, что угодно. Предположить, что в то августское утро в кабинете за столом напротив него сидел кадровый сотрудник советской разведки, он не мог даже в дурном сне.

— Я делал, что мог в то время, и был счастлив узнать однажды, что я зачислен в кадры советской разведки.

— Каким же образом, товарищ Ким, вам удалось попасть на службу в английскую разведку?

— Это довольно длинная история, — говорит он. — После окончания Кэмбриджа я некоторое время работал в одной

— Я пошел вверх по служебной лестнице. Через год я уже был заместителем начальника одного из отделов МИ-6.

— МИ-6, что это значит?

— В Англии существует две службы: под кодовым названием МИ-5 скрывается контрразведка. МИ-6 — это собственно секретная разведывательная служба.

— Западная пресса отмечала, что ва-

Он был внимателен в обращении с людьми, но по существу относился к ним свысока. В дела он не вникал, и, я бы сказал, при всей его агрессивности он был дилетантом, о чем лучше всего говорит авантюра с вторжением на Кубу, так позорно провалившаяся. Считаю, что он занял этот пост благодаря своему брату — Джону Фостеру Даллесу.

HERO'S WELCOME
Philby escaped to Moscow from Beirut, where he had been working under cover as a journalist. The Soviet newspapers welcomed him with banner headlines. This one reads "Greetings Comrade Philby."

Hammer and sickle, the symbol of the Soviet Union

COLD WAR MOLE
Harold "Kim" Philby (1912–1988) became a communist while he was studying at Cambridge University, and was a Soviet spy by 1933. Yet, seven years later, he had a job with Britain's MI6 intelligence service. After thirty years of spying he fled to Moscow. A grateful Soviet Union gave him a pension and a flat, the office of which is shown above.

MEDALS FROM BOTH SIDES
Philby received this plaque from the KGB soon after his arrival in Moscow. Later the Soviet Union gave him the Order of the Red Banner. Eighteen years before, England's King George VI, unaware that he was a spy, had given Philby the Order of the British Empire.

RETIREMENT IN MOSCOW
After defecting, Philby lived in Moscow until his death in 1988. His son took this photograph of him in the 1970s. The treachery of Philby and his fellow spies Guy Burgess and Donald Maclean left behind a trail of mistrust. Their espionage discredited the British intelligence services.

SECURITY SECRETS
As head of the KGB mission in London, Oleg Gordievsky (born 1939) had access to the most sensitive information about his country's espionage. Yet secretly he despised the Soviet system, and had been spying for the West since 1966. He defected to Britain in 1985 when his Soviet masters began to suspect him.

SECRET IDENTITY
Igor Gouzenko (1919–1982) was a cipher clerk in the Soviet Embassy in Ottawa. He did not wish to return to the Soviet Union, and defected with evidence of Soviet spying. He was turned away as a crank by newspapers and government departments, but the Mounted Police believed and protected him. For this TV interview he wore a hood to keep his identity secret.

Gordievsky with his book *KGB: The Inside Story*

Secret weapons

Espionage has a bloody past. Spies were busiest in wartime, when there was danger everywhere, and when war ended it was the job of intelligence organizations to make sure peace continued. Many wartime spies carried weapons openly, others disguised their guns and knives in often ingenious ways. With the Cold War (pp. 38–39) came greater secrecy. Both Warsaw Pact and Western powers attempted killings, and some, such as the murder of Georgi Markov, succeeded. Other schemes did not: the CIA twice tried, and failed, to kill Cuba's president Fidel Castro (pp. 42–43) with poison. The agency also considered more unusual weapons. They plotted to put deadly bacteria in Castro's cigar, and to blow him up with an exploding clam while he swam in the sea. But not all the agency's weapons would have been fatal. The strangest plot aimed to humiliate Castro. By putting special powder in the communist leader's shoes, CIA agents planned to make his distinctive beard fall out!

Pushing the trigger near the handle fired the pellet

DEADLY PENCIL
Disguised as pencils, these two weapons were used in close combat. The stabbing pencil contains a cross-shaped blade, and the propelling pencil fired a single chromium-plated bullet. Agents of Britain's SOE (pp. 32–33) used them to gain a brief advantage, so that they could seize more powerful weapons from their opponents.

Pencil is cut away here to show knife inside

Gun has no barrel limiting accuracy

Georgi Markov in 1978

UMBRELLA KILLER
The Bulgarian Georgi Markov broadcast, from the BBC in London, criticism of his country's leadership. Walking home over Waterloo Bridge one day in 1978, Markov felt a sharp pain. He looked round to see a man picking up an umbrella. Markov developed a fever, and died three days later. His assassin, a Bulgarian agent, had used a specially designed umbrella to fire a tiny pellet containing a powerful poison into Markov. Ten days earlier Bulgarian agents in Paris had attacked another opponent of the country's rulers, but the victim recovered.

Gas cylinder made umbrella work like air rifle

Holes in tiny pellet contained poison

Modified Webley & Scott 6.35 mm pistol

Shortened barrel

Trigger guard

GUN BELT
Worn on a belt under clothing, this small World War II pistol had a very short range. To be sure of a direct hit an assassin needed to be standing right next to the target. A firing cable from the buckle passed down the sleeve of the coat that covered the gun. The great advantage was that a spy could pull the trigger without anyone seeing him or her aim or fire.

SIMPLE SLASHERS

Not all weapons were aimed at people. These razor-sharp knives were designed to destroy vehicle tyres. They were small enough to hide easily, yet with a single slash an agent could gain valuable minutes in which to make an escape. Saboteurs used the knives to completely immobilize a vehicle by slashing all the tyres (including the spare).

Knife hung from thong around neck

Small slasher resembles ring

RING REVOLVER

Concealed weapons are nothing new. The well-equipped French spy of the 19th century carried this tiny revolver fixed to a ring. By revolving the chamber the agent could fire five shots. Because of its small size and firing method this design was sometimes called a squeezer pistol or palm pistol.

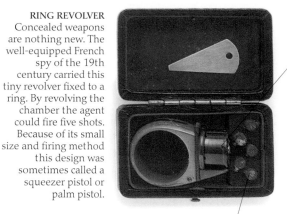

Because the pistol is so small, it had a very limited range

The ring gun can fire five bullets

LETHAL GLOVE

Some weapons used by spies appear more dangerous to the person using them than to the victim. An agent firing this ingenious glove pistol had to take careful aim as there was only one bullet and that could easily take off a couple of fingers. The United States Office of Naval Intelligence produced the gun for its World War II agents.

Barrel poked out between fingers

Pistol is riveted to a leather glove

Pressing the barrel against the victim's body fired the gun

Canadian maple leaf

HEEL AND COIN BLADES

Despite their vicious appearance, knives hidden in shoe heels were not intended for attack. Instead the concealed blades allowed agents who were tied up to cut themselves free. Spies also hid knives in low denomination coins. They hoped that their guards would let them keep the loose change in their pockets – even if the guards stole the banknotes.

Concealed blade

Concealed blade

Coin has a hidden blade

French tricolour

MESSY KNIVES

Wartime intelligence agencies designed these small knives so they could be hidden in a coat lapel or cuff. A captured agent could use the knife to attack guards and escape. Instructors who trained the spies warned that the results were often "messy".

The Cold War

W<small>HEN WORLD WAR II ENDED</small> in 1945, the future looked bleak for secret agents. In fact, a golden age of espionage was about to begin. A political boundary split Europe in two. Nicknamed the "Iron Curtain", it was actually just a line on a map. To the east lay the communist world – the Soviet Union and its allies - who wanted to create a classless society that shared everything. Nations to the west, supported by the United States, were capitalist, believing in the private ownership of property and businesses. Eastern and Western nations were deeply suspicious of each other, and their intense rivalry became known as the Cold War. Spies thrived in the atmosphere of mistrust that the Cold War created. They had plenty of work, with East and West racing each other to build the biggest bombs, and each side sending spies to discover what the other side was plotting. And because of all this activity, each side needed more counter-intelligence officers at home to catch enemy agents at work. On both sides of the Iron Curtain, fear of nuclear war meant that the money for spying never ran out. Finally, in 1989, the Cold War ended and the process of reuniting Germany, which had also been split in two, began.

HUNT THE MISSILE
Missile bases are easy to spot on photographs from spy satellites (pp. 52–53), so the United States and the Soviet Union developed submarine-based missile launchers which could hide beneath the waves. The designers of this Trident missile claimed it would be used to hit missile bunkers. Opponents believed that cities would be the real targets.

Distinctive mushroom-shaped cloud

TESTING THE BOMB
The United States tested its atom bombs in the Nevada desert, far from the prying eyes of enemy spies. The power of these bombs to destroy civilization frightened everyone, and may have gone a long way towards ensuring that neither side in the Cold War actually used one.

Crowds cheered as everyone with a hammer and chisel chipped at the wall

"KEEPING THE WORLD SAFE"
Politicians in the Cold War believed in "mutually assured destruction" (MAD). If each side had enough bombs to destroy the other, they reasoned, neither side would dare risk war. The two "superpowers", the Soviet Union and the United States, each built huge missiles with nuclear warheads. They never launched them, and these American Titan II missiles are in storage, waiting to be converted into satellite launchers.

THE WALL DIVIDING EUROPE
Cold War espionage was most intense in Berlin, the capital of East Germany. Berlin was situated well inside East Germany, but a wartime treaty gave France, Britain, and the United States control of West Berlin, so the city was itself divided into East and West. To prevent refugees escaping to the West across the new border, the East Germans divided the city of Berlin by building a wall in 1961. The wall's destruction by the people in 1989 united Germany, and symbolized the end of the Cold War.

EUROPE DIVIDED

In the Cold War, only four European nations were neutral. Most others signed pacts vowing to defend their neighbours. The Warsaw Pact united communist countries with the Soviet Union. Capitalist countries were allied with the United States as members of the North Atlantic Treaty Organization (NATO).

Map labels: Finland, Norway, Sweden, Denmark, Ireland, United Kingdom, Netherlands, Belgium, Luxembourg, East Germany, West Germany, Poland, Soviet Union, France (NATO member, but withdrew troops from NATO command in 1966), Switzerland, Austria, Czechoslovakia, Hungary, Romania, Yugoslavia, Italy, Bulgaria, Portugal, Spain, Albania, Greece, Turkey

BERLIN SPY SWAP

Any captured Cold War spies could expect execution or, at best, a long spell in jail – unless their government could negotiate a prisoner exchange. Under these deals, East and West swapped captured spies. The released agents walked to freedom at one of the checkpoints along the Berlin Wall.

SHOT DOWN

Before satellites simplified spying from above the ground, the United States sent U-2 spy planes (pp. 52–53) to photograph the other side of the Iron Curtain. The Soviet Union shot one down in 1960, and captured the CIA spy pilot, Gary Powers. He did not have to serve the ten-year sentence because the Soviets freed him in 1962 in exchange for Soviet spy Rudolph Abel.

U-2 pilot Gary Powers pictured after being shot down in 1960

Legend:
Iron Curtain
Neutral countries
Other capitalist nations
Full NATO members
Other communist nations
Warsaw Pact countries
Soviet Union

Graffiti added to remains of wall after reunification

BERLIN 1990

Spymasters

Espionage chiefs have enormous influence. The secrecy that surrounds all intelligence work means that, although most chiefs serve their country wisely, those that choose not to have dangerous powers. Usually spymasters take orders from a trusted group inside a country's ruling party, but often members of that party do not know what the spies are really doing. In the past, spymasters received their orders directly from the king or queen. However, in 1519 a Venetian diplomat wrote of the English King Henry VIII's first spymaster Cardinal Wolsey that he" …rules both king and the entire kingdom". In the 20th century, until the Cold War ended, secret service chiefs controlled whole Eastern European nations. J. Edgar Hoover's powers grew so great whilst he was the FBI chief that he was able to blackmail some of the most influential politicians in the United States. Countries are now more open about the existence of their security services, but the identity of agents in the spy networks is still a closely guarded secret.

ROMAN SOLDIER
General Scipio Africanus Major (236–184 BCE) was among the cleverest spymasters of the Roman Empire. While attacking the Spanish city of Carthago Nova, his spies discovered that the enemy's reinforcements were ten days' march away. As a result, the navy and army under Scipio's leadership won an easy victory.

POWER BEHIND THE THRONE
Cardinal Wolsey (1475–1530) became the most powerful man in England as the first head of intelligence services for King Henry VIII. Wolsey's agents opened the mail sent to diplomats from Venice and other nations. To protect their secrets, the ambassadors began to write their letters in code. Thomas Cromwell took over from Wolsey as controller.

Wolsey (left) had influence over the English king Henry VIII for many years

INDIAN INTELLIGENCE
Mogul ruler Akbar (1542–1605) united India. As a young king, he used fakirs (holy men) as spies. During his reign (1556–1605), Akbar extended the Indian empire, reforming the government. To do this he also relied on intelligence reports provided by *kotwal* (local officials), who had a duty to employ spies.

INVISIBLE SPIES
The warring princes of 12th-century Japan used *ninja* as spies and silent assassins. The ninja got their name from the Japanese word meaning "to make yourself invisible". They were trained to high standards of fitness, and were masters of disguise. One warlord, Takeda Shingen, so feared them that he fitted a second door to his lavatory to make escape easier.

RUSSIAN SECRET SERVICE
The first Tsar of Russia, Ivan IV (1530–1584) richly deserved his nickname "The Terrible". He ruled with the help of ruthless secret agents called the *Oprichniki*. Officially security police, the Oprichniki were really thugs who terrorized whole communities, killing and torturing without fear of punishment. They wore an emblem of a dog's head and a broom, symbolizing their powers to sniff out and sweep away treason.

Walsingham's cipher agents forged an extra paragraph asking Mary for the plotters' names

FATHER OF THE SECRET SERVICE
Francis Walsingham (about 1532–1590) did much to build up the English intelligence service. His greatest achievement was to uncover a plot to murder England's queen, Elizabeth I. Walsingham's agents intercepted coded letters between the plotters and the queen's imprisoned cousin Mary, Queen of Scots. The letters proved that Mary was involved, and she was executed in February 1587.

The letter was written in a simple code

A NEW BROOM SWEEPS CLEAN
For nearly half a century, J Edgar Hoover (1895–1972) was the head of the FBI, one of the functions of which was to detect enemy spies at work in the United States. Hoover's agents also snooped on the private lives of politicians, even the president himself. By threatening to make sordid secrets public, Hoover clung to his huge power. In 1947, the CIA was formed to deal with foreign security, and the power of the FBI was curbed.

THE RED CARDINAL
Cardinal Richelieu (1585–1642) organized the Cabinet Noir, a secret police force in France. His men spied on noble families, giving Louis XIII more power. The spies gained a reputation – every French teacher of sword-fighting was thought to be an agent.

SPY AT THE TOP
Alfred Redl (1846–1913) was Austria's chief spycatcher. He modernized the Austrian Secret Service but ran up huge personal debts. He was blackmailed into providing vital information for Russia, and accepted cash to work with them for ten years. Redl was accused of being a traitor in 1913, and shot himself rather than stand trial.

WOLF IN SHEEP'S CLOTHING
"The man without a face" was Markus Wolf's nickname during the Cold War. He was in charge of foreign operations for East Germany's Stasi (secret police). Wolf managed highly effective spy rings in the West. Even one of the close aides of the West German chancellor, Willy Brandt (1913–1992), had been recruited and was a Stasi spy.

The secret services

SPY VS SPY
Mad magazine's cartoon figures made fun of secret service rivalry at the height of the Cold War.

BEHIND EVERY SPY is a vast network for gathering intelligence. Organizations like the CIA and MI6 give spies documents, money, and help, and collect intelligence that the spies pass on. Intelligence networks interpret information not only from human spies, but also from a host of other sources. Satellites provide some of their data and interception of radio signals supplies more. Many of their staff do nothing but read foreign newspapers, magazines, and journals. A clever analyst can learn much from these "open sources". During World War II, Russian intelligence experts noticed the United States was hoarding silver for "scientific research", and had banned all atomic physics journals. Without putting agents' lives at risk, they guessed – correctly – that the United States was developing an atom bomb.

BEWARE OF SPIES
The Republic of China has a large but highly secretive intelligence network. There is a Ministry of State Security (MSS) that collects information, relying on different government organizations as well as the ordinary person in the street. In the 1970s, plaques such as this one (left) were posted all over the country to warn citizens against the activities of spies. Outside China, spies are believed to operate through the country's embassies and the New China News Agency.

Message reads: "At all times protect (our) secrets (and) everywhere guard against spies"

The emblem of the CIA

GUARDIANS OF THE UNITED STATES
The Central Intelligence Agency (CIA) has collected and analyzed foreign intelligence for the United States since 1947. It is also responsible for counter-intelligence abroad. The less well-known National Security Agency, which is under the control of the US Department of Defense (DoD), is actually bigger than the CIA, and handles signal intelligence – codes, ciphers, and the interception of communications. A separate organization, the United States Secret Service, has responsibility for protecting the president.

REGNUM DEFENDE

Badge of MI5, the counter-intelligence agency in Britain

THE STASI
Until Germany's two halves were reunited in 1990, the Stasi (State Security) handled intelligence for the East. East Germans had good reason to fear these secret police. The Stasi employed more than 85,000 people and had detailed files on a third of the East German population.

Badge worn by STASI officers who were not in uniform

SECURITY STAR
Britain has twin security agencies to handle intelligence and counter-intelligence at home (MI5) and abroad (MI6). In 1992, Britain was the first country to appoint a woman, Stella Rimington, as the head of a major intelligence agency. Until 1995, she was director of MI5, also called the Security Service, and originally formed in 1906. MI6 is the military name for the Secret Intelligence Service, and staff refer to its shadowy director as "C".

Map showing the Soviet Union

ISRAELIS SPYING ABROAD
Israel has developed ruthlessly efficient security and intelligence services. Formed in 1949, Mossad (the Institution for Intelligence and Special Services) is responsible for foreign espionage and taking action against the country's enemies. Shin Beth (Security and Counter-espionage Service) handles internal security.

A menorah – the symbol of Judaism

Badge of the PGU, the Soviet foreign intelligence office before 1991

Badge of Mossad

Vanunu's desperate message about his kidnapping in Rome

SPYING FOR RUSSIA
The SVR (Foreign Intelligence Service) was created in 1991 following the collapse of the Soviet Union. It became responsible for collecting intelligence outside Russia. Counter-intelligence (domestic spying) activities and all other internal intelligence activities were grouped together as the Federal Security Service (FSB). Combined, the SVR and FSB are much larger than the old KGB during the Cold War.

MOSSAD AT WORK
Agents of Mossad are particularly skilled at undercover work in foreign countries. In 1986, when Mordechai Vanunu, a senior nuclear technician, revealed that Israel was building atom bombs, Mossad agents kidnapped him in Italy and took him back to Israel to face trial and imprisonment. When in Israeli custody, Vanunu wrote a message for the press on his hand, giving details of the kidnapping.

TARGET PRACTICE
Despite what you see in movies and on television, the work of intelligence services rarely involves assassination. Spies want secrets, not dead bodies. During the 20th century, the Russian KGB (Committee of State Security) actively conducted multiple assassinations internationally while the CIA became famous for its fanciful but unsuccessful plans to assassinate Cuban leader Fidel Castro.

Manurhin 7.65 mm pistol

PROTECTING FRANCE
Like many other nations, France divides its intelligence work among several organizations. The Direction Générale de la Sécurité Extérieure (DGSE) collects foreign intelligence and organizes counter-intelligence abroad. The efficient Direction de la Surveillance du Territoire (DST) is controlled by the Ministry of the Interior and handles internal security. In the early 1980s, the DST was directly responsible for the expulsion of 47 Soviet diplomats suspected of spying.

DGSE agents abroad defend themselves with automatics like this

Surveillance at work

SPIES COULD BE WATCHING YOU. Business secrets are potentially valuable to rival companies, and to obtain those secrets, subterfuge is often used by employees or outside agencies. To steal documents, industrial spies use the tools and methods of a secret agent, and to protect the same documents from snoopers, businesses must adopt counter-intelligence tactics (pp. 48–49). The devices shown here all help protect office secrets from intruders. However, all of them can also monitor employees, for the espionage threat may come from inside the company. Workplace spies can watch low-paid staff who may be bribed to sell information to rivals. The spies aim to catch disgruntled managers wiping computer discs. Even office gossip can be a target for hidden microphones: it may warn that senior staff plan to leave and set up in competition.

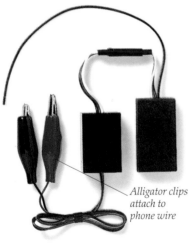

ARE YOU RECEIVING ME?
Business people can learn a lot about their clients with a tiny bug like this. A sales representative making a presentation can "accidentally" leave a bugged folder in the conference room to record a client's private conversation.

SITTING COMFORTABLY
As more business is done over the Internet, spies realize the importance of secretly accessing a person's emails and computer files for information about their financial dealings, projects, and personal life. Robotic spy software can be emailed to a target's computer disguised as a photo, music file, or a greeting card. Once inside, the software infects the computer and sends secret copies of the user's emails and files to the spy over the internet.

Alligator clips attach to phone wire

BUGGING THE WORKPLACE
An ordinary office desk telephone is an ideal hiding place for a bug (above). It has a built-in power supply and clips to the telephone line somewhere out of site ready to pick up any conversations.

LOUD AND CLEAR
A sales representative who has planted a bug is able to eavesdrop on his client from a car parked outside. By pulling up the radio antenna, he can pick up the signal and listen to any discussion of the sales pitch. The following day, the sales rep can return to negotiations, able to use the information to change strategy, and ready to bargain.

PINHOLE PEEPER
More than one in every ten American companies use video cameras to spy on their employees. Concealing the cameras is simple: the smallest have lenses that are much smaller than a match-head.

CAUGHT ON CAMERA
FBI agents used a hidden video camera in 1979 to collect evidence in a corruption case that they nicknamed "ABSCAM". The video (above) proved that members of Congress (the United States parliament) were taking bribes. Seven members of Congress were convicted and went to jail.

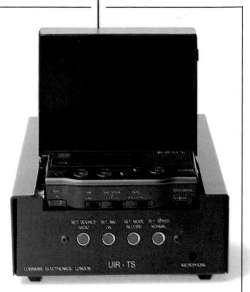

INFINITY RECEIVER
Most office bugs have a limited range but infinity receivers use the telephone lines to allow eavesdropping from anywhere in the world that there is a telephone. The "spy" must first install the device, usually attached to the telephone line. The bug does not operate until the spy dials the number of the bugged telephone, followed by a specially-selected key on a touch-tone telephone. The bug detects the tone, and stops the target phone from ringing. Then it allows the spy to hear a conversation in the room, using the telephone mouthpiece as a microphone. With the infinity receiver, it is possible for someone in Sydney, Australia, for example, to eavesdrop on conversations in Washington DC.

USB connector plugs into computer

THANKS FOR THE MEMORIES
A USB flash stick is a memory storage device with a universal connector that works on almost any computer. About the size of your thumb, it is easily hidden and can be used by a spy to secretly copy hundreds of thousands of pages of documents stored inside a computer network. Most intelligence services have removed the USB connectors from their computers to prevent theft of their documents.

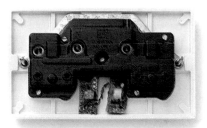

BUG IN A PLUG
Disguised as a wall socket, a bug is impossible to detect without taking the socket apart or using special equipment. The socket functions normally, and also supplies the bug with power. Some devices work like baby alarms, using the mains power cables – instead of radio waves – to transmit signals. The spy monitors any conversations with a suitable receiver plugged into any other socket on the same circuit.

ROBOTIC EYES
Although usually associated with street surveillance, some offices have monitoring rooms where security officers use closed circuit television cameras (CCTV) to watch and protect employees as well as reporting suspicious activity. Cameras are connected to large digital storage devices and the internet. If a spy can learn the company's secret computer password he can monitor activities from anywhere in the world.

Industrial espionage

GOVERNMENTS AND POLITICIANS are not the only targets of espionage. Businesses also have secrets which industrial spies try to steal or copy. This kind of espionage is rapidly expanding, but it is hardly new. The silk industry was an early victim. Until the 6th century, only the Chinese knew how to make this luxurious cloth. Then the Byzantine emperor Justinian I (483–565) used espionage to steal the secret of its production. He encouraged two monks to smuggle silkworms out of China in hollow canes. Industrial spying is more sophisticated today, but governments still encourage it if their nation benefits. In 1989, the French Department of Commerce planned to steal trade secrets from American and British companies. The spying became public when an informer posted their "shopping list" to the CIA. Usually, though, it is businesses that use industrial espionage against their competitors. Successful spies find design details, lists of suppliers and buyers. Even advance knowledge of a price list can help squeeze a competitor out of business.

SPYING ON THE COMPETITION
One of the most common forms of industrial espionage is for trusted employees to quit and join a competitor – taking secrets with them. General Motors (GM) suspected Jose Ignacio Lopez do Arriortua of doing this when he left to join rivals Volkswagen. GM claimed that de Arriortua and other executives left GM with thousands of photographs and plans of the Opel Vectra which was then secret. There have been similar scandals in Formula 1 racing car design. In 2007 McLaren was fined for possessing confidential Ferrari information.

Computer-aided designs of new cars are fiercely protected from industrial espionage

General Motors' Opel Vectra

In Europe billions of pounds are lost each year through audio, software, and DVD piracy

Long before they emerge on the catwalk, designs of evening dresses are the target of spies

THE ENTERTAINMENT INDUSTRY

Piracy (illegal copying) and industrial espionage cut the profits made by people in the world of entertainment. From a single original, pirates can make millions of CDs or DVDs. Security at recording and film studios must be intense to make sure that master tapes are protected until the scheduled release date. Despite these precautions, industrial spies occasionally succeed in smuggling out a recording: pirates made thousands of illegal copies of the James Bond film *Casino Royale* and distributed them throughout Asia before the film's London première.

To keep shape of new car secret, it can be disguised by fitting new parts in old car bodies when road-testing

Revolutionary disc braking systems may interest rival car manufacturers

COSTUME DRAMA

Theft of ideas and designs in the fashion industry is big business. It is easy to claim and often difficult to prove. Cutters and other workers in the garment trade might copy patterns and sell them to another designer. It is also possible to recreate designs from sketches or photographs taken at designer dress shows.

INDUSTRIAL DIAMONDS

An industrial spy at General Electric earned more than $1 million for passing secrets of synthetic diamond manufacture to a South Korean company. By stealing the knowledge they needed to build the plant, the Koreans avoided paying licence fees for the technology, and in addition saved the enormous expense of funding a research and development programme. General Electric discovered the espionage in 1992.

Tiny synthetic diamonds in drill's tip help it cut faster

COMPUTER SPYING

In 1981, the FBI caught a computer engineer, Kenji Hayashi, with secret details of IBM computer disc drive technology. His employers, Japan's Hitachi corporation, gave him more than half a million dollars which he used to bribe IBM staff. After his arrest and trial, Hitachi had to pay IBM 60 times this sum in compensation.

Counter-intelligence

IN THE PAST, bugging equipment was often simple, and wires from hidden microphones sometimes led directly to eavesdropping spies. Today, finding bugs and wiretaps – and spies who use them – is harder, especially as much of it is conducted over the internet. It is the job of counter-intelligence agencies to track them down. However, detection of spies does not always lead to their capture – sometimes an enemy spy is more valuable if allowed to carry on as normal. Working spies can provide a counter-intelligence agency with useful information, especially if they do not know they are being watched. A spy's activities can give away secrets about spying techniques and equipment. These details can be used to help trap other spies. Counter-intelligence services also use unmasked spies to feed false information to their enemies. Sometimes, by confronting spies with evidence of their guilt, a counter-intelligence agency can force the spies to work against their original masters as double agents.

SOMEONE IS WATCHING YOU
Counter-espionage agencies use many of the same tools as the spies themselves. This 19th-century cartoon makes fun of the craze for hidden cameras among spies and counter-spies alike.

KEEPING CALLS SECRET
During the Cold War, portable scramblers were sometimes used to keep telephone calls private. A typical scrambler breaks up speech into short segments, then rearranges these into an apparently random order for transmission down the telephone line. The receiving scrambler reverses the process. The people talking hear each other perfectly, but a spy who taps the line will hear nothing but "grey noise" (a meaningless jumble of sound). Modern digital scramblers utilize software with built-in encryption to protect conversations sent over the internet against eavesdropping.

Cold war scrambler attached to telephone

SETTING THE CODE
A caller uses a row of tiny switches to set their scrambler to the same prearranged code as the receiving scrambler.

COUNTER-SPY'S TOOLKIT
When checking for bugs, the counter-spy uses screwdrivers and other basic tools to undo plug casings, and look behind light sockets and other likely places. A visual inspection can reveal damage left when a bug was installed. And by comparing every cable with a wiring diagram a counter-spy can confirm whether there are cables linking microphones to a distant transmitter.

Rising tone in headphones indicates presence of a bug

Handle is removable to aid search of cramped spaces

Reducing power output helps pinpoint hidden bugs

Probe detects bugs even when they are not transmitting

A NEW BROOM
This device is used by a counter-intelligence officer to quickly sweep (check) a room for bugs. The probe gives off a radio signal, which energizes semi-conductor devices, such as transistors or integrated circuits. This creates a tell-tale signal which the "broom" detects. Innocent electronic devices such as telephones will activate the detector, but once these are taken into account, any remaining signals probably come from a concealed bug.

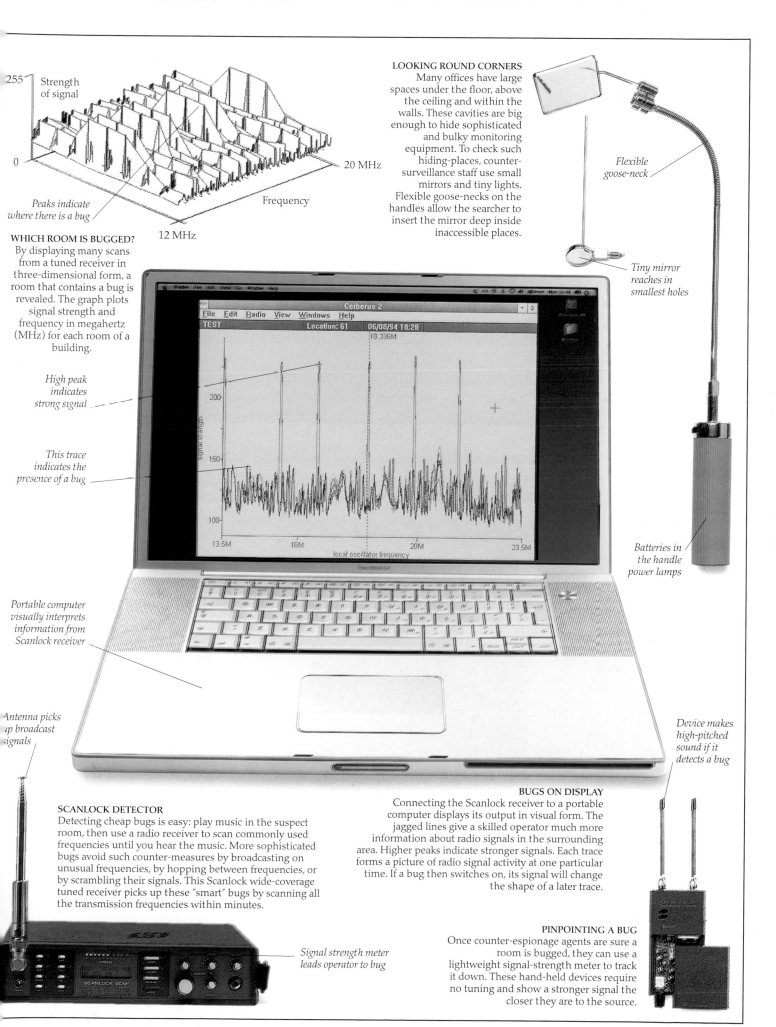

255

Strength
of signal

0

*Peaks indicate
where there is a bug*

12 MHz

20 MHz

Frequency

LOOKING ROUND CORNERS
Many offices have large spaces under the floor, above the ceiling and within the walls. These cavities are big enough to hide sophisticated and bulky monitoring equipment. To check such hiding-places, counter-surveillance staff use small mirrors and tiny lights. Flexible goose-necks on the handles allow the searcher to insert the mirror deep inside inaccessible places.

*Flexible
goose-neck*

*Tiny mirror
reaches in
smallest holes*

WHICH ROOM IS BUGGED?
By displaying many scans from a tuned receiver in three-dimensional form, a room that contains a bug is revealed. The graph plots signal strength and frequency in megahertz (MHz) for each room of a building.

*High peak
indicates
strong signal*

*This trace
indicates the
presence of a bug*

*Batteries in
the handle
power lamps*

*Portable computer
visually interprets
information from
Scanlock receiver*

*Antenna picks
up broadcast
signals*

*Device makes
high-pitched
sound if it
detects a bug*

SCANLOCK DETECTOR
Detecting cheap bugs is easy: play music in the suspect room, then use a radio receiver to scan commonly used frequencies until you hear the music. More sophisticated bugs avoid such counter-measures by broadcasting on unusual frequencies, by hopping between frequencies, or by scrambling their signals. This Scanlock wide-coverage tuned receiver picks up these "smart" bugs by scanning all the transmission frequencies within minutes.

*Signal strength meter
leads operator to bug*

BUGS ON DISPLAY
Connecting the Scanlock receiver to a portable computer displays its output in visual form. The jagged lines give a skilled operator much more information about radio signals in the surrounding area. Higher peaks indicate stronger signals. Each trace forms a picture of radio signal activity at one particular time. If a bug then switches on, its signal will change the shape of a later trace.

PINPOINTING A BUG
Once counter-espionage agents are sure a room is bugged, they can use a lightweight signal-strength meter to track it down. These hand-held devices require no tuning and show a stronger signal the closer they are to the source.

Spy-catching

Intelligence officers leave court carrying Bossard's spying equipment

LOCATING AND IDENTIFYING SPIES is rarely easy – unless a mole or defector betrays them. Suspicious radio signals can sometimes allow counter-intelligence agents to pinpoint a hidden transmitter. By tapping telephones and secretly opening mail a counter-spy can find a few, and patient surveillance catches many more. Careless spies can give themselves, and others, away when collecting intelligence. For example, following a suspected spy sometimes leads to the discovery of other unknown agents. Once they are caught they must be "neutralized" – this means exposing them so they cannot work secretly, expelling them to their home country, or prosecuting and imprisoning them. In some countries neutralization can have a more sinister meaning – an unfair trial and a death sentence.

BLEEPS TRACE MISSILE SECRETS
A tip-off by a defector alerted Britain's MI5 to spy Frank Bossard (born 1912). They caught him by fixing a transmitter to the files he "borrowed" from his Air Ministry office. The beacon's radio bleeps led MI5 officers to where the spy was copying the documents.

Probe fits through slit at top of envelope and jaws grip the letter

SUSPICIOUS SPY-CATCHER
As counter-intelligence chief of the CIA, James Jesus Angleton (1917–1987) hunted spies for two decades. He trusted nobody, and suspected every defector of being a KGB double agent. He found few moles, however, and his intense suspicion slowed the agency's work. By ordering illegal mail interceptions he damaged his reputation and was sacked in 1974.

Winding handle rolls letter into tight coil

Applying invisible crayon sticks powder to a surface

By pulling handle agent pulls out letter

The Rosenbergs are taken from court after being convicted

FLAPS AND SEALS
Counter-espionage agents use tools like this to open letters, read them and replace them without tearing the envelope. This skill, known as "flaps and seals", allows them to monitor letters addressed to a spy. Letters posted by the spy, however, are much more difficult to intercept.

ROUGH JUSTICE
Harsh punishment of spies has sometimes aroused strong emotions. Julius and Ethel Rosenberg were caught giving secrets to the Soviet Union. They were the first American spies sentenced to death during peacetime and many people begged for mercy for them. Despite this, they were convicted for their espionage during World War II, condemned, and finally died in the electric chair in 1953.

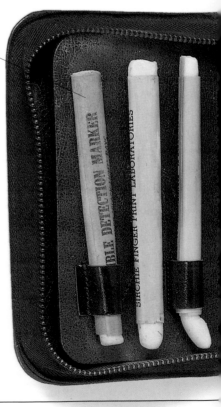

CAUGHT IN THE ACT

Video surveillance can catch a spy at work, but checking tapes from many cameras is very time-consuming. New digital cameras linked to surveillance software (see pp. 44–45) can recognize faces and identify known spies in a crowd of people even if they are disguised. Once spotted, the computers will automatically track and record the spy's movements while alerting security officers.

Surveillance cameras can be used to track a suspect's movements

MERSH agent's identity card

Ultraviolet light shows up anti-bugging seals

"DEATH TO SPIES"

The Soviet counter-espionage organization Smert Shpionam (roughly translated as "death to spies") was responsible for military security, and for catching spies within the country's intelligence services. The agency soon acquired the nickname "SMERSH".

CHECKING SEALS

After a bugging sweep counter-intelligence agents use seals to secure "clean" areas. An ultraviolet lamp is used to show up the anti-bugging stickers to check they are not broken.

RED-HANDED

By dusting secret files with these special powders (left), counter-intelligence agents can catch a spy who handles the material. Powder sticking to the spy's hands glows under light from sources such as the ultraviolet lantern (above right).

RFID chip transmits radio waves over a range of more than 90 m (295 ft)

CHIPS WITH EVERYTHING

RFID (Radio-Frequency Identification) chips only slightly larger than the full-stop at the end of this sentence are called "taggants" and can be attached to a person's clothing, shoes, or even a passport or ID card and used to secretly track his movements. Security services, such as Britain's MI5, use RFID chips in London to monitor foreign spies posing as diplomats.

Powder is invisible in normal light when sprinkled on files

Spying without spies

SPY PLANES WITHOUT PILOTS
Darkstar is a drone, or uncrewed aerial vehicle (UAV), developed in the United States. UAVs can take detailed air photographs of heavily defended enemy territory without risking a pilot's life.

THE WORK OF REAL LIVE SPIES – or HUMINT (human intelligence) – is both costly and slow, and if a spy is discovered this could embarrass politicians. Fortunately there are some alternatives. Technical intelligence-gathering uses remote sensors which can do the spy's work from a distance. COMINT (communications intelligence); SIGINT (signals); ELINT (electronic) and IMINT (imagery) all provide valuable knowledge. Perhaps the most important is IMINT, which is the gathering of pictures from cameras and radar in spy aircraft and satellites. These provide amazing views of objects on the ground – some can even distinguish between civilians and soldiers. Just as satellites improve a spy's distant vision, technical intelligence far below makes other senses keener. Sea-bed hydrophones track the sound of enemy submarines and, like sensitive fingertips, seismographs detect the vibrations caused by atomic tests.

SPY SATELLITE LAUNCH
Older spy satellites used film because the pictures produced were sharper than video. The film fell to Earth in a capsule for collection and processing. Such spy satellites are still secret. This Soviet launch carries a civilian version into orbit.

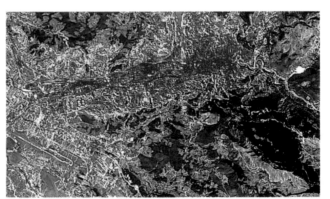

Russian KFA satellite on ground after re-entry

SEEING EARTH FROM SPACE
Multi-spectral images give intelligence agencies very detailed pictures of war zones and military bases, but they do not show the landscape in true colours. In this image of Sarajevo in former Yugoslavia, electronic processing has made buildings stand out in pink. With greater enlargement, pictures can record objects as small as a truck.

Sensors behind coloured windows view targets in both visible light and infrared

Engines power the Blackbird forward three times faster than the speed of sound

EYES IN THE SKIES
American Keyhole 12 spy satellites can see objects as small as a grapefruit from a distance of 400 km (250 miles). No nation releases pictures of its spy satellites. However, this Earth observation satellite, which is used for map-making, is built in the same way. Radar imaging allows spy satellites to look straight through cloud cover and infrared sensors can even pick out heat shadows left by a missile launch. Multi-spectral cameras in the satellite make it possible to distinguish between real trees and camouflage.

Aircraft is very light in weight to increase range

Cockpit is not pressurized: pilot breathes pure oxygen from a helmet

U-2 SPY PLANE
The CIA welcomed this high-flying spy plane as a triumph when it first flew in 1955 because they believed it was more accurate and dependable, and could collect information faster, than any agent on the ground. The U-2 could cruise well above 19,810 m (65,000 ft), but this proved not high enough when a Soviet missile shot down one in 1960. The pilot was captured (pp. 38–39).

Explosion was equivalent to an earthquake with a magnitude of 6.2 on the Richter scale

ground up

TRACING THE BIG BANGS
Seismographs make vibrations in Earth's crust visible as a trace on paper. Geologists normally use them to monitor earthquakes, but the instruments can also register underground nuclear tests on the other side of the world. In September 1949, United States intelligence analysts got their first firm evidence that the Soviet Union had developed the atom bomb from a trace like this one.

Trace shows activity at the Soviet Union's Kazakhstan test site in central Asia

TAKING A CLOSE LOOK
This is a unique photograph taken in 1984 of a Soviet aircraft carrier under construction in a Black Sea shipyard. The picture shows the ship's hull being built in two separate sections. Computer enhancement and colour have improved the quality of the picture.

Black paint is needed to dissipate heat, because friction with the atmosphere warms the plane to 427°C (800°F)

BLACKBIRD WITH SHARP EYES
The *Blackbird* reconnaissance plane was built to replace the U-2. Though designed in 1959, the two-seater still flies higher and faster than any other aircraft. It can cross the Atlantic in less than two hours, and photograph a country the size of Mexico in 13 hours. Lockheed developed the U-2, the *Blackbird*, and *Darkstar* at a top-secret plant in Burbank, California, known as the "Skunk Works", later moving to Palmdale, California. *Blackbirds* collected intelligence for more than 20 years during the Cold War, but were mothballed (taken out of service) to save money in 1990. Five years later, the US Air Force reconditioned several of them, and once more began training aircrew to fly surveillance missions.

SKY HIGH EYE
Satellite data helps environmentalists monitor climate change and loss of habitat because of human activity or natural disaster. Spy satellites take the sharpest pictures, but until recently these have been kept secret. Now the US makes its images available to the general public. They will give researchers a clearer picture of how Earth has changed over the last 40 years.

Spying today

SPIES THRIVED IN THE COLD WAR. While it lasted the United States and the Soviet Union feared each other's bombs and missiles, and needed intelligence agencies to help keep the peace. Initially, when the Cold War ended in the late 1980s, many spies lost their jobs. Intelligence agencies had to adapt quickly. They looked for new uses for their spy technology and some formed alliances with the scientific community. Technology developed for global surveillance was adapted for use in other areas. Besides tracking submarines, America's secret hydrophone network listened in to the sound of whales. Today, intelligence services still use the hydrophones, along with advanced satellites to keep track of enemy submarines. Earth observing satellites, once reserved for intelligence agencies, are now run by private companies. Intelligence agencies found that their skills in catching spies were just as useful in identifying terrorists. Intelligence officers who had trailed Cold War traitors now followed Colombian drug barons. However, the relative quiet period for intelligence services that came in the immediate aftermath of the Cold War, in the early 1990s, gradually abated. Now the Russian intelligence service, as well as the CIA, is much larger than it was during the Cold War.

DRUGS ON THE STREET
Intelligence agencies can collect information about the production and the smuggling of narcotics. However, the war on drugs does not end when shipments reach their destination. Kits like these (left) help agents catch drug dealers. The sprays quickly identify drugs wherever they are, avoiding the cost and delay of laboratory analysis.

EVERCHANGING ROLE
However much the world changes, there will always be a role for secret agents. The danger of war in Eastern Europe has largely disappeared only to be replaced by war and political instability in the Middle East. US Secret Service agents also have an important role to play guarding the president.

US Secret Service man protects President Bush at an anti-drug summit

DRUGS SNOOPER
The war against drugs increasingly relies on American satellites that were once used to police nuclear weapon treaties. High above Colombia, a "spy in the sky" can identify jungle landing strips, drug laboratories and storage areas. Using information gathered by satellite pictures, Colombian soldiers swoop on the bases with helicopters and ground troops. They have seized vast amounts of cocaine in single raids.

Shoulder bag conceals a machine-gun

54

*Fuel rod contains
pellets of nuclear
material*

*Plutonium sealed
inside is highly
poisonous, but
radiation it emits
is not a danger to
bomb-makers*

FUELLING FEAR

Terrorists need 7 kg (15.5 lb) of plutonium from a nuclear power plant to build a bomb, and workers in Russia's crumbling nuclear industry are happy to sell it. Intelligence services across the world cooperate in tracing this stolen plutonium and uranium.

SHINING PATH

Behind bars, Abimael Guzman no longer leads the Shining Path guerrilla movement that terrorized Peru for more than 20 years, killing 25,000 people. Police used spy tactics to catch him in 1992, first collecting intelligence, and then staking out his apartment with agents in disguise.

ORGANIZED CRIME

In the United States, the FBI tracks spies and fights organized crime gangs such as the Mafia and Chinese Triads. Counter-intelligence and security organizations, such as MI5 in Britain, have only recently joined the police in the fight.

Gamblers gather at the headquarters of New York's Hung Mon Association, which has direct links with Triad gangs

*Receiving aerial collects
incoming radio signal*

*Transmitting aerial
can direct signal
back to multiple
destinations*

SPY IN THE SKY

Satellites with powerful digital cameras are able to photograph objects as small as 75 mm (3 in) from space and transmit instant pictures back to intelligence services. Events can be analyzed as they are happening to provide current information to military and national leadership, by departments such as the National Reconnaissance Office (NRO). But who has access to that information? In 2001 former NRO employee Brian Regan contacted the Iraqi government just before the invasion and offered to sell US satellite secrets revealing US knowledge of the locations of Iraqi weapons.

Spying and you

YOU ARE UNDER SURVEILLANCE! Every day, cameras capture you walking along the street and the journeys you make in your car. Your cellphone calls and the sites you surf on the Internet are logged by communications providers, and your shopping purchases are recorded by supermarkets and stores. And it's not just you – the same goes for every other member of the public. Governments around the world are also busy compiling databases on their populations, from people's medical records and identifying features to details of their financial dealings. Such monitoring helps to make our countries and neighbourhoods more secure, our health services more efficient, and our leisure time more rewarding – but it also comes with the potential for misuse.

CAUGHT ON CAMERA
For many people, CCTV proved its worth in the aftermath of the terrorist bombings in London on 7 July 2005. CCTV footage showed the bombers on their way to the capital on the morning of the attack, and also on a reconnaissance trip to London nine days before the blasts (above). The footage enabled the police to identify the bombers within hours of the attack.

Cameras can be remotely controlled to pan, tilt, and zoom in for a closer view of targets

Operator can select a camera and use it to investigate anything that seems "unusual"

CCTV MONITORING CENTRE
London contains more CCTV cameras (*see* p.45) per square kilometre than any other city. Police officers sit in front of vast arrays of television monitors connected to public and private surveillance cameras throughout the London area. The CCTV cameras are linked to large-capacity digital storage drives, where the images are labelled with a date/time stamp and archived for future study. In some CCTV systems, an operator can "mark" a suspicious individual, who is then tracked automatically from camera to camera. Civil liberties groups complain that people should be able to go about their daily lives without being under constant surveillance, but the authorities argue that CCTV makes criminals beware and the streets safer.

EYES AND EARS OF THE POLICE
Many roads and streets are under constant watch by CCTV cameras. Some cameras record traffic flow and read car number plates, others monitor pedestrians. Multiple microphones mounted on CCTV towers can also listen for problems such as gunshots. The directions from which sounds reach the microphones are used to calculate the position of the shot and guide police to the scene.

Touch-screen shopping trolley for RFID-tagged goods

WE KNOW WHAT YOU BUY...

Instead of marking products with bar codes, some stores use RFID tags (*see* p.51). When placed in a shopping trolley, the tag on the product is detected by an on-board receiver. RFID purchases are logged by the store's database and used to order new stock. The data can also be used to analyse people's spending habits. There are concerns that the tags may one day be able to be traced to the customer's home, which some people see as a threat to their privacy. Stores dismiss these worries, saying that the tags would be deactivated at the shop's exit.

TODDLER TRACKERS

Toy-like beacons, such as the Giggle Bug Toddler Tracker® shown here, can be used by parents to prevent their toddlers from getting lost. Containing an RFID tag, the tracker makes a bleeping sound when a parent presses the button on the hand-held fob, revealing the child's location within a 30-m (100-ft) radius. Similar devices using Global Positioning System (GPS) chips allow companies to track their laptop computers and locate key employees as they travel around. Such technologies could also be used to monitor a person's movements without their knowledge.

Pressing the fob reveals whereabouts of child

Giggle Bug Toddler Tracker®

Ladybird tag clips on to child's clothes

Computer scanner records iris pattern

IRIS SCANNING

Biometric data such as fingerprints, DNA samples, and iris scans can be used to identify people – trusted individuals, criminals, and terrorists alike. Each person has unique patterns of blood vessels on their irises (the coloured rings around the eyes' black pupils). An iris scanner analyses these patterns and compares them to those on a database to see if there are any matches. In theory, biometric data could also be used by the state to keep tabs on civilians it considers politically troublesome.

ONLINE PERILS

Every time you visit a website, you unknowingly leave a telltale sign known as a "cookie". These details can be used to compile data on your Internet activity. Downloading files that have not been checked for viruses may allow a hacker to secretly access private information on your hard drive, and even remotely turn on your web cam without your knowledge. Social networking sites like Facebook and MySpace allow you to link with like-minded people anywhere. But be careful – not everyone is truthful, and your new online "buddy" might be predator lurking in disguise.

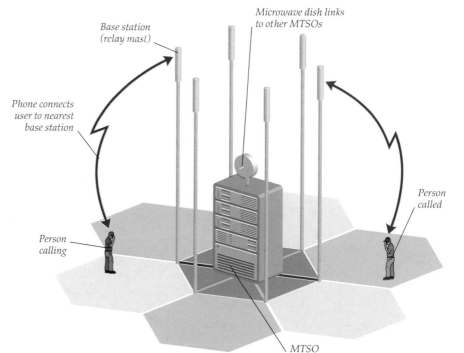

Microwave dish links to other MTSOs

Base station (relay mast)

Phone connects user to nearest base station

Person calling

Person called

MTSO

MOBILE PHONE TRACING

A cellphone (mobile phone) company divides the area it serves into a grid of hexagonal "cells". Each base station (relay mast) is located at the point where three cells meet. Two people talking on the phone are each connected to their nearest base station. The base stations are linked via an MTSO (Mobile Telephone Switching Office). The phone company's log shows which base stations took part in the call and their relative signal strengths. This information can be used by emergency services and police to calculate a user's position to within 38 m (125 ft).

Famous spies

THE MOST SUCCESSFUL SPIES do not become famous. As soon as their work is complete, they disappear into the shadows. Wartime spies are the exception to this. When the fighting ends, they tell their stories and sometimes earn high honours. As a reward for her spying, and for enduring torture and imprisonment, Odette Sansom received one of Britain's most important medals, the George Cross. Not everybody believed that she deserved it. Yvonne Cormeau (pp. 32–33) complained that other SOE agents got a lesser award because "we haven't been caught". Of course all spies try to avoid capture, but if it happens, fame can follow quickly. Their captors are eager to put the spies' crimes on show. Spy trials often disappoint newspaper readers who follow them – in a real spy's life glamour is rare, and the routine boring. However, a few spies do live lives as exciting as any novel. Some actually turn into fictional characters: Ian Fleming based James Bond on the spy Dusko Popov.

Sean Connery as Bond in the film of *Dr No*

WILL THE REAL SPY STAND UP?
Fictional James Bond in the first Bond film, 1962, (top) and real spy Dusko Popov (above with his wife) both enjoyed gambling and the company of beautiful women. Bond's creator, Ian Fleming (pp. 60–61) met Popov in 1941 when Fleming was a British naval intelligence officer.

For her stage act, Mata Hari wore elaborate costumes and headdresses, but often danced naked as well

Mata Hari falsely claimed to be the daughter of a temple dancer and that she had been dedicated to the god Shiva

FAILED SPY
As Mata Hari, exotic dancer Margaretha Macleod (1876–1917) entertained German officers in France during World War I. Although she became one of the most famous names in the history of espionage, she was not very good at spying. She was recruited by the German Secret Service, but they did not entirely trust her, and she offered her services to the Allies. Germany finally betrayed her to France and on 15 October 1917, she was executed by a French firing squad.

CODENAME "WHITE RABBIT"
Welsh Royal Air Force officer "Tommy" Yeo-Thomas became famous after his arrest and torture by the Gestapo, the German secret police, during World War II. He had been working for the SOE (pp. 32–33), organizing the French resistance to German troops occupying France. He was betrayed and captured outside a metro station in Paris. Tortured by the Gestapo, he was imprisoned but escaped from the death camp at Buchenwald in Germany.

Forged papers gave "White Rabbit" cover stories on his visits to France

Donald Maclean (1913–1983) passed atom bomb secrets to Moscow

Guy Burgess (1911–1963) attracted attention with his drunken violence

Kim Philby (1912–1988) warned Maclean and Burgess when to flee

Anthony Blunt (1907–1983) helped the others escape to the Soviet Union

Odette Sansom was the first woman to win the George Cross

Odette Sansom with the dolls in 1954

Dolls entirely hand-sewn

Ski sticks made from card and silver foil

WARTIME HEROINE

During World War II, Odette Sansom (1912–1995) worked as "Céline", an agent for the Allied Special Operations Executive (SOE). She helped organize resistance groups in southern France. Betrayed by a double agent in 1943, Odette was captured and taken to Fresnes Prison near Paris where she was horribly tortured. After Fresnes, she was transferred to a prison in Germany and then to a concentration camp. Making these dolls for the nephew and niece of a German Catholic priest helped her pass the long hours of captivity. She was finally freed by the Allies in May 1945. The cruelty of her ordeal, and the valour with which she faced it have made her a legendary wartime spy.

THE CAMBRIDGE FIVE

Four of the 20th century's most notorious spies met at Cambridge University, England. While working for Britain's Foreign Office, Guy Burgess and Donald Maclean leaked secrets to Moscow, fleeing there in 1951 when MI5 began to suspect them. When the "third man" Kim Philby (pp. 34 – 35) joined them in 1961, a "fourth man", Anthony Blunt, secretly admitted to spying. In return for his confession, Blunt kept his job as Surveyor of the Queen's Pictures until he retired. However, by 1979, his name had become public knowledge and, later, a "fifth man", John Cairncross, was revealed.

SHOW TRIAL VICTIM

Soviet military intelligence officer Oleg Penkowsky (1919–1963) contacted Western intelligence agencies in 1960. He believed he could prevent war by telling the West about Soviet nuclear missiles. The secrets he provided gave the United States a real advantage in the Cold War. The KGB caught Penkowsky and he was given a show trial at which he "confessed". He was sentenced to death and reportedly executed in 1963.

Spies in fiction

Michael Caine played Harry Palmer in the 1965 film version of The Ipcress File

ESPIONAGE HAS ALL THE INGREDIENTS for an exciting storybook or movie: suspense, action, intrigue, and natural drama. American author James Fenimore Cooper (1789–1851) helped establish the spy story with his book *The Spy* in 1851, but spy novels have only really become popular in the last 50 years. Some of the most successful authors were themselves spies. Ian Fleming worked for British naval intelligence during World War II. John Le Carré drew on his experience of MI5 and MI6 to create a more authentic picture of the secret agent's world. Hollywood turned the books of both authors and many more into successful movies, but the books and films did not always impress real spies. Allen Dulles, once head of the CIA, wrote that "spy heroes… rarely exist in real life". This did not stop the CIA from using spy films to train agents on the finer points and pitfalls of their trade.

ANTI-HERO
In *The Ipcress File*, writer Len Deighton created a spy hero who shared only his nationality with James Bond. The story of the Cockney petty criminal turned reluctant spy was Deighton's hugely successful first book.

AUTHOR MEETS SPY
Frederick Forsyth (left) based his book *The Odessa File* on the exploits of the German "Champagne Spy" Wolfgang Lotz (right). Lotz crippled the Egyptian missile programme, helping Israel win the Six Day War against Egypt in 1967.

Lotz's high lifestyle earned him his nickname of "the Champagne Spy"

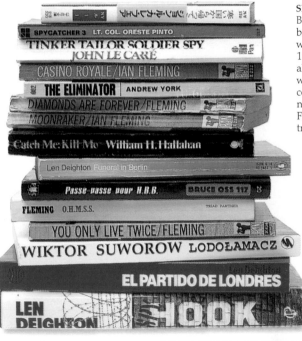

SPY HIT LIST
British spies may not be the world's best, but the country's espionage writers top the best-seller lists. In the 1960s, their anti-Communist message alarmed the KGB. The Soviets hit back with *The Zakhov Mission*, in which a communist hero defeats 007. It could not compete with the success of Fleming's originals, which have been translated all over the world.

FICTIONAL EVIL LADY
"We are enveloped in a network of spies," cries D'Artagnan, the young hero who helps the three musketeers in the famous adventure story written by Alexander Dumas (1802–1870). Milady (right) is the most deadly of the spies who are employed by Cardinal Richelieu (pp. 40–41) to try and discredit the Queen of France.

Bond uses a piton gun to fire rope during a spectacular bungee jump in the opening sequence

Grappling hook at end of rope

INDIAN ROPE TRICK

High-tech gadgetry is as much the star in a Bond film as 007 himself. In the Bond books, Ian Fleming based these devices on genuine inventions supplied by people such as Charles Fraser-Smith to World War II agents (pp. 10–11).

Buckle conceals 27-m (75-ft) long fine rope which can bear Bond's weight

Telescopic sights

Bond's belt worn in the film *Goldeneye*

TIME TOOL

Watches play a leading role in many of the Bond films. In *Goldeneye*, a laser built into Bond's watch helps him cut his way out of difficult situations. The KGB studied James Bond films in order to develop their own spy technology.

James Bond's piton gun from the film *GoldenEye*

Piton gun contains laser which Bond uses to cut open the roof of a Russian chemical plant

LICENSED TO PRINT MONEY

When Ian Fleming (1908–1964) created the character of James Bond, he was aiming to write the spy story "to end all spy stories". He succeeded. The 14 Bond books sold more than 18 million copies.

In GoldenEye, *the seventeenth James Bond film, Pierce Brosnan plays the sophisticated British spy*

Bond destroyed the chemical plant using a magnetic mine

The buggist's true-to-life tool kit includes a lock-pick gun

BUGGED BATHROOM

In the film *The Conversation*, a bugging expert (played by Gene Hackman) is drawn into a terrifying world of deception and murder. As nerve-racking as any political spy story, the film is a rare and authentic glimpse of industrial espionage at work.

Rogues' gallery of spies

SOME SPIES WORK FOR DECADES without discovery, but if a spy is uncovered and put on trial, it often makes headlines and he or she becomes a figure of public hate. Occasionally, spies manage to escape from prison or the clutches of counter-intelligence officers and flee to the country for which they spied. There they are celebrated as daring adventurers, but in the country where they spied they remain not just rogues but vile traitors who put the nation's security, business, and people at risk.

ABEL, RUDOLPH
A KGB mole (*see* p. 9), Abel was the KGB's chief agent in the USA until he was arrested in 1957. He was swapped in 1962 for US pilot Gary Powers, who had been shot down over the Soviet Union in 1960. Abel was given a hero's welcome in Moscow, and spent the rest of his life teaching KGB trainees.

AGEE, PHILIP
Codenamed "Pont", Agee was a CIA officer who worked covertly for Cuban intelligence and the KGB. He revealed the names of 2,000 undercover CIA officers, including Richard Welch, the CIA chief in Greece. This led to the murder of Welch outside his home. Agee died in Cuba in 2008.

BARNETT, DAVID H
In 1976, former-CIA-officer Barnett began selling secrets to the KGB to pay off debts, including details of HA/BRINK, a CIA operation that collected information on weaponry given by the Soviets to Indonesia. Barnett also betrayed the identities of more than 30 CIA officers.

BELL, WILLIAM H
William Bell worked on radar at the Hughes Aircraft Corporation in California, USA. Faced with financial difficulties, he agreed to sell radar secrets to Marian Zacharski, a Polish intelligence officer. In 1981, Bell was confronted by FBI agents. He confessed, and helped the FBI to catch Zacharski.

BLAKE, GEORGE
While a senior intelligence officer for MI6, George Blake was also spying secretly for the KGB because he believed in the principles of Communism. Blake was betrayed by a Polish defector in 1961. He escaped from Wormwood Scrubs Prison, London, in 1966, and eventually made his way to Moscow, where he took up residence.

Rudolph Abel

George Blake

BOYCE, CHRISTOPHER J
A US defence industry employee, Boyce and his friend Andrew Doulton Lee were arrested in 1977 for selling satellite secrets to the Soviets, which they passed to KGB officers in Mexico. Boyce later escaped from prison, but was recaptured after 19 months on the run.

CARNEY, JEFFREY M
Carney, a US Air Force intelligence specialist, spied for the East German HVA (foreign intelligence service) while stationed in West Germany. He carried on spying on his return to the USA, but in 1985 defected to East Germany. Carney was arrested by US counter-intelligence officers two years after the collapse of the East German state.

COHEN, ELI
This Egyptian-born linguist was recruited by Israeli intelligence to infiltrate Syria's ruling Baath Party. He supplied Israel with information about the Syrian military and its fortifications on the strategically important Golan Heights. Cohen was arrested in 1965 and executed.

CONRAD, CLYDE L
A retired US Army sergeant, Conrad was arrested in West Germany in 1988 for passing classified material to Hungarian intelligence, including NATO plans for the defence of Europe. He is thought to have been aided by at least a dozen other army personnel – one of the biggest spy rings since World War II.

GIMPEL, ERIC
In 1944, during World War II, a German submarine landed Gimpel and fellow German spy William Colepaugh on a beach in Maine, USA. The spies went to New York, where they lived the high life using the money intended for their espionage. Colepaugh turned himself in to the FBI and helped them to catch Gimpel.

HAMBLETON, HUGH
In 1956, Hambleton, a Canadian economist for NATO, was recruited to the KGB because of his access to top-secret documents. His motivation was not money, but the belief that his spying would help to create world peace. He was arrested while holidaying in London in 1982.

HANSSEN, ROBERT P
An FBI counter-intelligence officer, Hanssen began spying for the Soviets in 1979. He betraye details of US security programmes and even the location of the underground bunker where the US government would be housed in the event of a nuclear war. His information also led to the execution of three US agents in Russia. In 2001 Hanssen was arrested in Vienna, Virginia, USA, while trying to hide secret FBI documents.

HERRMANN, RUDOLPH
This KGB mole entered the US from Canada in 1968, and spied while posing as a photographe He acted as a courier for the KGB, transmitting material collected by other spies. After his arres by the FBI in 1977, Hermann worked as a double agent until his mission ended in 1980.

HOWARD, EDWARD L
In 1983, Howard was forced to resign from the CIA after failing a lie-detector test when quizze about theft and drug use. Two years later he wa revealed as a KGB spy by Soviet defector Vitaly Yurchenko. Howard eluded his FBI surveillance and fled to the Soviet Union.

ISMAYLOV, VLADIMIR M
In 1986, Ismaylov, a Soviet military attaché stationed in Washington, DC persuaded a US Air Force officer (really an FBI undercover agent) to supply him with secret military data. He was detained at the drop-site in Maryland. Because of his diplomatic status, he could not be tried, so he was expelled from the USA.

Robert P Hanssen

KHOKOLOV, NIKOLAI
A Soviet intelligence officer, Khokolov trained as an assassin in 1953. His first target was the Russian leader of an anti-Soviet political party based in West Germany. Khokolov's weapon was a pistol fitted inside a gold cigarette case. Instead of carrying out the job, he defected to th US, where he revealed much about the Soviet murder programme. Khokolov himself narrowl survived poisoning by Russian agents in 1957.

KOECHER, KARL F
In 1965, Karl Koecher, a Czech mole, and his wife Hana staged a phoney defection to the US where Koecher later obtained a job with the CIA translating top-secret materials. Until his arrest in 1983, he passed classified information to the KGB and Czech intelligence, including the names of CIA agents. He was exchanged fo Soviet dissident Anatoly Shcharansky in 1986.

LONSDALE, GORDON
From 1955 to 1961, when he was arrested by MI5, Lonsdale was the chief Soviet mole in Britain. His real name was Konon Molody, but he posed as a Canadian businessman. Lonsdale was part of a spy ring that revealed details of Britain's underwater weapons systems. In 1964, he was exchanged for Greville Wynne, a British agent being held by the Soviets.

MERCADER, RAMÓN
Spanish-born Mercader was trained as an assassin by the Soviet intelligence service. In 1940, he was sent to Mexico City to kill Leon Trotsky, the exiled opponent of Soviet dictator Josef Stalin. Mercader visited Trotsky's home to ask him to review an article he had written for a newpaper. While Trotsky read the piece, Mercader hit him in the head with an ice axe, and he died the next day. After 20 years in a Mexican prison, Mercader returned to Moscow a hero.

MICHELSON, ALICE
In 1984, Michelson, an East German, was arrested when boarding a plane from New York to Czechoslovakia with tape recordings hidden in a cigarette packet. Michelson was acting as a courier for Soviet intelligence. Before her case came to trial, she was exchanged along with three other East European spies for 25 people imprisoned in East Germany and Poland. It was the biggest ever "spy swap".

MONTES, ANA B
Montes was motivated to spy by her political beliefs, rather than money. She was recruited as a Cuban spy in 1984, while still at college. She began work in the US DIA (Defense Intelligence Agency) in 1985, and provided top-secret information to the Cuban intelligence service until her arrest in 2001.

NICHOLSON, HAROLD J
On his arrest at Dulles International Airport, Washington, DC, in 1996, Harold Nicholson was found to be carrying rolls of film bearing images of top-secret documents. Nicholson, the highest ranking CIA officer ever charged with espionage, began spying for Russian intelligence in 1994. For two and a half years he hacked into the CIA's computer system and provided the Russians with every secret he could steal.

NORWOOD, MELITA
The longest-serving Soviet spy in Britain, Melita Norwood began spying in 1938. When working as a typist for a company involved in Britain's top-secret project to develop an atomic bomb, she supplied nuclear secrets to the Soviet Union. Norwood was not revealed as a spy until 1999, when she was 87. Because of her age, the British authorities decided not to prosecute her.

PITTS, EARL E
In return for payments totalling $224,000, FBI special agent Pitts gave classified material to first Soviet and then Russian intelligence services between 1987 and 1992, including a list of FBI informants in Russia. Pitts was unmasked with the help of his wife Mary, who told another FBI agent of her suspicions.

POLLARD, JONATHAN J
Arrested in 1985, Pollard was a US naval intelligence analyst and Israeli spy. He provided so much top-secret information to his Israeli handlers that they had to set up a high-speed "copy shop" in the home of an Israeli staff member, using the latest photocopying machines.

REGAN, BRIAN
In 2001, Regan, a retired US Air Force sergeant, was arrested in Washington, DC, while attempting to board a plane bound for Switzerland. A ciphered message was discovered inside his shoe. It took months to decode, but it finally revealed the locations where Regan had buried 21 caches of secret US documents. Regan, who was heavily in debt, had tried to contact the Iraqi dictator Saddam Hussein to demand $13 million for information about US reconnaissance satellites.

REILLY, SIDNEY
A Russian-born adventurer who spied for MI6 during the Russian Revolution of 1917, Reilly "Ace of Spies" was a master of disguise who posed as a member of the Cheka, the Russian secret police. Once, fearing arrest, he tore up secret documents he was carrying and swallowed them. Reilly later went to live in New York, but in 1925 he was persuaded by the British to return to Moscow, where he was caught and executed.

RITTER, NICHOLAS
In the years before World War II, Ritter, a German military intelligence officer, developed agents in the USA and Britain. His greatest success came in 1937, when his agent Herbert Lang supplied him with top-secret plans for the Norden bomb sight, an aiming device that allowed high-altitude aircraft to drop their bombs with precision. The plans were cut up and the pieces mailed to Germany inside newspapers.

SCRANAGE, SHARON M
While working for the CIA in Ghana in 1983–84, Scranage revealed the identities of CIA informants and agents to the Ghanaian intelligence service. The Ghanaians passed on the damaging information about CIA intelligence gathering activities to Libya, Cuba, East Germany, and other allies of the Soviet Union. Scranage came under suspicion in 1985, when she failed a routine lie-detector test on her return to the USA.

Jonathan J Pollard

SHADRIN, NIKOLAI
A Soviet naval officer who defected to the US, Shadrin (real name Nikolai Artamanov) was forced by the FBI to become a double agent in 1966. When Shadrin visited Vienna, Austria, in 1975, he was abducted by KGB officers and was accidentally killed in a struggle with his captors.

TREHOLT, ARNE
The head of the Norwegian Foreign Ministry's press office, Treholt was arrested while boarding a flight from Norway to Austria with a suitcase full of classified documents for the KGB. A search of his home revealed a further 6,000 pages of secret NATO material. Treholt had first come under suspicion in 1980, when he was part of Norway's delegation to the United Nations.

Arthur James Walker

WALKER, ARTHUR J
Beginning in 1980, Walker, a retired US Navy lieutenant-commander, passed information about the design and construction of US warships to his brother John (see p. 8), a KGB spy, while working for a defence company in Virginia. The Walker spy ring, which also included John's son Michael and Jerry Whitworth (below) was one of the most damaging in US history.

WHITWORTH, JERRY ALFRED
A collaborator with the Walkers (above), Jerry Whitworth gave the Soviets information on US naval communications between 1975 and 1982. The "key lists" that he supplied, along with details of the Navy's cryptographic equipment, enabled the Soviets to decode US naval messages. John and Michael Walker testified against Whitworth in return for a lesser sentence for Michael Walker.

Harold J Nicholson

Ana B Montes

Timeline of modern spying

THERE HAVE ALWAYS BEEN SPIES, but the early 20th century marked the start of a "golden age" of spying, as powerful nations came head to head in the political arena and on the battlefield. In particular, the Cold War era following World War II saw unprecedented levels of espionage, with the USA and the Soviet Union vying for supremacy on the world stage.

1909
The British Secret Service Bureau is set up. It will later give rise to MI6, the agency for protecting and promoting British security overseas.

1917
Mata Hari is executed in Paris after a trial in which she is used as a scapegoat to blame French military failures on enemy spies.

1917
Founding of the Cheka (Russian Security and Intelligence Service) in St Petersburg. Under the Soviets, the Cheka will later become the KGB.

1918
The Soviet Union forms the Chief Intelligence Directorate of the General Staff (GRU) to focus on the collection of military information abroad.

1923
German engineer Arthur Scherbius exhibits his Enigma ciphering machine, which Germany will use for secret communication in World War II.

1929
In 1929, Henry L. Stimson, the US Secretary of State, closes the US Cipher Bureau, proclaiming "Gentlemen do not read each other's mail."

1939
World War II begins, with the invasion of Poland by the forces of Nazi Germany.

1940
Leon Trotsky, the exiled opponent of Soviet Union dictator Josef Stalin, is murdered in Mexico, having been tracked by Stalin's spies for 12 years.

1940
Britain forms the Special Operations Executive (SOE). Prime Minister Winston Churchill orders its head, Hugh Dalton, to "set Europe ablaze!"

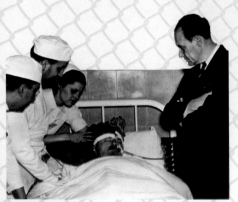
Leon Trotsky lies dying in a hospital bed, 1940

1941
The USA creates the COI (Coordinator of Information), the world's first centralized intelligence service.

1941
Caught unaware, the USA suffers a devastating attack by Japanese aircraft on Pearl Harbor and other naval bases in the Hawaiian islands. The attack is a major failure by US intelligence.

A US warship burns in Pearl Harbor, 1941

1941
Soviet spy Richard Sorge warns Stalin of German plans to attack Russia, but he is ignored. He also accurately predicts Japan's invasion of the Dutch East Indies to replace its dwindling oil reserves.

1942
The US creates the Office of Strategic Services (OSS) to succeed the COI.

1943
The British attach mock "secret plans" to a dead body and let it wash up on a Spanish beach. The plans convince the Germans that the Allies are planning to invade the Balkans and Sardinia instead of the island of Sicily, the real target.

1943
Russian scientist Lev Sergeivich Theremin converts a light bulb into a listening device by targeting it with a radar-like signal. It can pick up all conversation taking place around it.

1943
The Allies meet in Tehran, Iran, to plan the last phase of the war against Germany. The Soviets use bugs to eavesdrop on the US delegation and learn of their secret negotiating positions.

1944
The world's first programmable electronic computer, Colossus, is used at Bletchley Park, England, to decipher German communications in advance of the D-Day invasion.

Colossus computer at Bletchley Park, 1944

1945
World War II ends in victory for the Allies, but in its aftermath the Cold War begins. The West is separated from the Soviet Union and its Communist allies by the military, political, and ideological barrier known as the Iron Curtain.

1945
Captured German Enigma cipher machines are repaired by the British and later presented to other nations for use in secret communications. The countries that receive them are not told that the British can decipher the messages they send.

1945
Harry Truman, US Vice President, succeeds Theodore Roosevelt as President. Truman learns for the first time of the secret US atomic bomb project. The Soviet leader Josef Stalin already knows of the secret thanks to his spy networks.

1947
US President Harry Truman establishes the Central Intelligence Agency (CIA).

1947
Soviet intelligence successfully eavesdrops on every foreign embassy in Moscow.

1949
The Soviet Union tests its first atomic bomb years ahead of Western expectations, due to the successful theft of atomic secrets from the West.

1950
US Senator Joseph McCarthy causes anti-Communist hysteria by alleging that the US government is heavily infiltrated by Communist spies. Decades later Soviet spy archives will reveal that, though exaggerated, the claims are at least partly true.

1952
In Moscow, a wooden eagle plaque given to the US Ambassador in 1945 by Russian "Young Pioneers" (boy scouts) is found to be bugged. Every word spoken in the Ambassador's office has been heard by the Soviets for seven years.

1953
After an uprising believed to have been stirred up by Western intelligence, East Germany forms its secret police, the Ministry for State Security (Stasi).

1953
Julius and Ethel Rosenberg, two American Communists, are executed for passing nuclear weapons secrets to the Soviet Union in wartime.

1955
The CIA and MI6 build a spy tunnel under the streets of Soviet-occupied East Berlin to tap into a communication cable between Soviet military forces and Moscow. MI6 officer George Blake, a KGB double agent, gives information that enables the Soviets to "discover" the tunnel in 1956.

1956
First flight over the Soviet Union by the new US high-altitude U2 spy plane.

1959
The first Corona satellite is launched, one of a series of satellites used by the CIA to photograph the Soviet Union, China, and other areas.

1960
A CIA U2 spy plane piloted by Francis Gary Powers is shot down over the Soviet Union.

1961
Because of Cuba's close links with the Soviet Union, US President John F Kennedy authorizes an invasion. A CIA-armed and -trained force (the 2506 Brigade) lands at the Bay of Pigs. The Cubans easily fight off the invasion.

1963
In the UK it is revealed that John Profumo, Secretary of State for War, has had an affair with the showgirl Christine Keeler, who was also involved with a Russian naval attaché and GRU intelligence officer).

1963
The CIA offers a pen containing a poison-filled hypodermic needle to a Cuban agent to assassinate Cuban leader Fidel Castro. It is never used.

1963
Ex-MI6 officer Kim Philby is revealed as a KGB agent. He escapes to the USSR.

1967
US naval officer John Walker volunteers as a Soviet spy. During the next 17 years, Walker's information will enable the Soviets to decipher over a million secret messages.

1972
Sir Anthony Blunt, former Surveyor of the Queen's Pictures, is revealed as having been a KGB spy from the 1930s to the 1950s. He was one of the "Cambridge Five" (see p.59).

1974
A US vessel posing as a deep-sea drilling platform recovers part of K-129, a Soviet submarine that sank in 1968 in 5,120 m (16,800 ft) of water.

1978
Aided by the KGB, Bulgarian agents kill Bulgarian dissident Georgi Markov in London, jabbing him with a poison-tipped umbrella.

1979
FBI agent Robert Hanssen walks into the Soviet American Trading Organization in New York City and offers to spy for the Soviets.

1980
CIA disguise expert Tony Mendez invents a fake Canadian movie project and travels to Iran to check out filming locations. He brings six US hostages out of Iran disguised as part of his film crew.

1981
Turkish gunman Ahmet Ali Agca shoots and wounds Pope John Paul II in Rome. Italy accuses the Bulgarian secret service of being behind the shooting.

1985
KGB Colonel Oleg Gordievsky, a mole for MI6, escapes from Moscow while under surveillance by the KGB's 7th Directorate.

1985
KGB Commander Vitaly Yurchenko defects to the CIA in Rome and is secretly flown to the US. He soon re-defects, claiming that he had been kidnapped and drugged by the Americans.

1985
CIA officer Aldrich Ames offers to work for the KGB. He reveals all US sources inside the KGB, resulting in at least 10 deaths.

US President John F Kennedy, who authorized a CIA-backed invasion of Cuba in 1961

The sinking of the *Rainbow Warrior*, 1985

1985
France's foreign intelligence agency, the DGSE, sinks the Greenpeace ship *Rainbow Warrior* in New Zealand, to prevent it from obstructing a French nuclear test in the Pacific Ocean.

1986
A defector alerts the CIA to the use of "spy dust" (nitrophenylpentadienal, or NPPD) by the KGB in Moscow to track the movements of suspected CIA and MI6 officers posing as diplomats.

1986
Israeli dissident Mordechai Vanunu travels to London with photos of Israel's secret nuclear programme. He is lured to Rome by "Cindy", an Israeli agent posing as a US tourist, then drugged, taken back to Israel, and imprisoned.

1989
The Berlin Wall, which has divided Berlin since 1962, is torn down.

1991
The Soviet Union breaks up, marking the end of the Cold War and the Iron Curtain. The now-defunct KGB's foreign-intelligence activities will be taken over by a new Russian agency, the SVR.

1992
Former KGB archivist Vasili Mitrokhin defects to the UK, revealing that he has buried thousands of secret notes under his house near Moscow.

1999
FBI agent and SVR mole Robert Hanssen tells the Russians of a secret eavesdropping tunnel under the Russian embassy in Washington, DC.

1999
SVR officer Stanislav Gussef is arrested outside the US State Department in Washington, DC, where he has secretly bugged a conference room.

2003
The US and its allies invade Iraq, saying that it has "weapons of mass destruction". Much of the evidence used to justify the invasion, from Iraqi defector Rafid Ahmed Alwan, turns out to be false.

2006
Alexander Litvinenko, former lieutenant-colonel of Russia's Federal Security Service (FSB), dies in London of radiation sickness. Russian agents are suspected of causing his illness.

2006
Russia claims that British spies have been sending secret information using a transmitter hidden inside a fake rock on a Moscow street.

The end of the Berlin Wall, 1989

Find out more

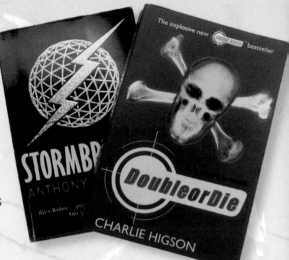

As well as gathering information from secret sources, intelligence officers use "open sources", such as newspapers, television news, and Internet blogs. Today, the Internet is the largest store of open-source information. Many of the tools used by intelligence officers (such as the Internet search engine Google™) are available to you on your home computer. So start discovering more about spying by going online. You can learn espionage skills on visits to spy-themed museums, exhibitions, and leisure attractions. Novels and movies can also give an entertaining (if not authentic) flavour of the secret life of spies.

Spies on film

James Bond (007) is the world's most famous movie spy. Created by writer Ian Fleming in 1953, he was featured in 12 novels, although more than Bond 20 films have been made to date. The movie series began in 1962 with *Dr No*; recent Bond movies include *Casino Royale* (2006) and *Quantum of Solace* (2008).

Recently, Bond's popularity has been rivalled by a new character, Jason Bourne. The movies *The Bourne Identity* (2002), *The Bourne Supremacy* (2004), and *The Bourne Ultimatum* (2007) were adapted from novels by Robert Ludlum. They feature the escapades of Jason Bourne, a CIA intelligence officer who has lost his memory.

Many purists who understand the real nature of espionage consider the best spy film to be *The Spy Who Came in from the Cold* (1965), based on John le Carré's novel of the same name.

Scene from Austin Powers spy-spoof film

As well as action heroes, there have been comedy spies, including Austin Powers, who made his debut in *Austin Powers: International Man of Mystery* (1997), and *Johnny English* (2003) – a spoof of James Bond.

Films for children include *Spy Kids* (2001), *Spy Kids 2: Island of Lost Dreams* (2002), and *Spy Kids 3-D: Game Over* (2003). These movies feature the adventures of Juni and Carmen Cortez, children of superspy parents. Alex Rider, the teenage boy forced to join MI6, made the leap from the novel to the big screen in 2006 with the movie *Stormbreaker*.

INTERNATIONAL SPY MUSEUM
The world's largest public spy museum is located in Washington, DC, USA. Visitors to the International Spy Museum first learn the skills of espionage and then see how famous (and not so famous) spies have secretly influenced world events. Spy fiction is also covered here: James Bond's Aston Martin DB5 car from the movie *Goldfinger* (1964) is one of the museum's most popular attractions.

SPY BOOKS
Few spy novels are realistic: espionage is actually about secretly and methodically gathering information useful to your government, rather than thrill-a-minute, explosion-filled adventures. But spy novels can be entertaining nevertheless. Among the spy books for young readers are Charlie Higson's stories about the young James Bond, such as *Double or Die* (2007) and *By Royal Command* (2008), and Anthony Horowitz's tales of the teenage superspy Alex Rider, which include *Stormbreaker* (2000) and *Snakehead* (2007).

Exhibits at the International Spy Museum, Washington, DC, USA

Cryptanalyst's headphones and message transcripts at Bletchley Park, UK

BLETCHLEY PARK MUSEUM
In World War II, Bletchley Park, near Milton Keynes in the UK, was the headquarters of British intelligence and the centre of its code-breaking activities. Among the exhibits are reconstructions of the Bombe, the machine used to break Germany's Enigma codes, and Colossus, the world's first programmable electronic computer, which cracked the codes of Lorenz, another German cipher machine. The collection also includes cipher machines from the Cold War period.

Enigma machines at the National Cryptologic Museum, Maryland, USA

Examining bugging devices at Spymasters in Cambridge, UK

NATIONAL CRYPTOLOGIC MUSEUM
Located next to headquarters of the National Security Agency at Fort George G. Meade, Maryland, USA, this museum contains thousands of artefacts that trace the dramatic role cryptology has played in US history. Visitors learn about the people who devoted their lives to cryptology, the machines and devices they developed, the techniques they used, and the places where they worked.

TEST YOUR SPY SKILLS
There is a growing number of leisure attractions where you can get hands-on experience of spy equipment, acquire some spy skills, and see how you fare as a spy in role-play scenarios. At Spymasters, in Cambridge, UK, visitors undertake missions to steal secrets from a mocked-up foreign embassy, taking care to avoid detection by alarms, sensors, and cameras.

Glossary

AGENT A person who works for, but is not officially employed by, an intelligence service.

AGENT IN PLACE An agent recruited by an intelligence service who already works for the target organization.

AGENCY An intelligence service or a body responsible for some aspect of national security.

ASSASSIN Someone who murders a politically important person, either for money or other rewards or for political reasons.

BUG A hidden microphone, often linked to a transmitter, for secretly listening to conversations.

CCTV (Closed-Circuit Television) Video cameras used to transmit signals to a specific, limited set of monitors. The signal is not openly broadcast, as in normal television. CCTV is widely used for security surveillance.

CHEKA (Russian abbreviation for Extraordinary Commission for the Struggle against Counter-revolution, Espionage, Speculation, and Sabotage) Cheka was the Russian secret police, founded in 1917. It eventually gave rise to the KGB.

CIA (Central Intelligence Agency) The US agency responsible for world-wide intelligence gathering and counter-intelligence abroad.

CIPHER A type of code that cannot be understood without access to a secret "key" for decrypting messages.

Cheka identity card

CODE A system for conveying messages by systematically substituting letters, numbers, or symbols for the original text of a message.

COLD WAR The state of conflict, tension, and competition that existed between the United States and the Soviet Union and their allies between 1945 and 1991.

COMINT (Communications Intelligence) Information derived by intercepting communications between people, via phone taps, mail tampering, and room bugs.

CONCEALMENT Hiding messages, ciphers, bugs, or other espionage materials in specially adapted everyday objects.

COUNTER-ESPIONAGE Operations to penetrate a hostile foreign intelligence service.

Camera concealed in a book

COUNTER-INTELLIGENCE A broad term that includes actions against foreign intelligence services, and the protection of people, information, equipment, and installations from espionage, sabotage, and terrorism.

COURIER A person who carries secret material for an intelligence service, either knowingly or unknowingly.

CRYPTANALYSIS Also known as code-breaking, this is the study of ciphers and other kinds of codes to reveal their hidden messages.

DEAD DROP A hiding place, usually in a concealed container, used for secret communication and exchange of material between a spy and his or her handler.

DEFECTOR A person who, by choice, leaves a country and flees the control of its intelligence service in order to serve the interests of another country.

DGSE (*Direction Générale de la Sécurité Extérieure*) France's external intelligence service, similar in function to Britain's MI6 and the USA's CIA.

DOUBLE AGENT An agent of one intelligence service who is recruited and controlled by another intelligence service, and who secretly works against their original service.

ELINT (Electronic Intelligence) Information obtained by intercepting machine-to-machine electronic communications, such as by spy aircraft "listening" to enemy radars.

ENIGMA An electromechanical cipher machine used by the German military and government for ciphering and deciphering messages in World War II. Cracking the Enigma codes was vital to the Allies' success in World War II

ESPIONAGE Using spies to obtain secret or confidential information about the plans and activities of a foreign government, a competing business, or other organizations.

FBI (Federal Bureau of Investigation) The agency responsible for counter-intelligence and other law-enforcement duties within the United States.

FLAPS AND SEALS A term for opening, examining, and resealing envelopes and packages without raising the suspicion of the recipient.

GESTAPO (Abbreviation of *Geheime Staatspolizei*) Founded by the Nazi Party, the Gestapo was Germany's secret police in World War II, responsible for internal security.

GRU (Russian abbreviation for Chief Intelligence Directorate) Founded in 1918 as the Russian military intelligence service, the GRU survived the fall of the Soviet Union in 1991 and has continued serving the state of Russia.

HANDLER An intelligence officer who is responsible for, or controls, an agent.

HUMINT (Human Intelligence) Information directly collected by agents themselves, as opposed to information collected by equipment and technology.

Briefcase containing a concealed flaps and seals kit, 1960s

HYDROPHONE A device designed to be used underwater for recording or listening to sound.

ILLEGAL An agent operating in a foreign country without diplomatic protection, but with a false identity. An illegal usually has no contact with his or her own embassy, and is controlled by intelligence services in their own country.

IMINT (Image Intelligence) Intelligence in the form of images gathered by cameras and radar on spy aircraft and satellites.

INDUSTRIAL ESPIONAGE The secret acquisition of information about business. It may be carried out by a competing firm or by an intelligence officer.

Badge of America's NSA

MORSE CODE An internationally recognized code that substitutes sequences of dots and dashes for letters and numbers.

MOSSAD (Hebrew abbreviation for Institute for Intelligence and Special Operations). Mossad is Israel's foreign-intelligence gathering agency.

NATO (North Atlantic Treaty Organization) A military alliance, originally established during the Cold War, made up of countries from North America and Western Europe.

NEUTRALIZE To render a spy ineffective, such as by exposing them publicly so they cannot work secretly, expelling them to their home country, or prosecuting and imprisoning them.

NSA (National Security Agency) The US agency responsible for protecting government information and communications, often by encryption. It also collects and analyses foreign signals, often by cryptanalysis.

OPERATIVE An officer or agent operating under the control of an intelligence service.

PICKLOCKS Specially shaped tools that enable the user to unlock doors without a key.

PLANT A spy who works his or her way into a target organization in order to collect intelligence.

RECEIVER An electronic device that receives signals from a transmitter.

RECONNAISSANCE A mission undertaken to secure information, usually in advance of a secret operation.

RFID CHIP (Radio-Frequency Identification chip) A tiny computer chip that transmits radio signals. RFID chips can be embedded in passports and ID cards to prevent identity fraud. They are also used on some supermarket goods to monitor purchases, and as secret "tags" by some security services to track the movements of known spies.

SABOTAGE Covert actions that weaken an enemy or opponent through the destruction of property or the disruption of essential services.

SCRAMBLER A device that prevents telephone tappers from understanding a conversation, often by rearranging the words spoken.

SIGINT (Signals Intelligence) A broad term that refers to intelligence obtained by intercepting enemy signals. It includes COMINT and ELINT.

SPY An agent used by a state to obtain secret information about enemies, or someone employed by a business to obtain confidential information about its competitors.

INFORMER Someone who reveals secret or confidential information, often for money.

INTELLIGENCE The profession of espionage, the information collected by espionage, or the final analysed product.

IRON CURTAIN The military, political, and ideological barrier that existed between the countries of the West and the Soviet Union and its Communist allies from 1945 to 1991.

KGB (Russian abbreviation for Committee for State Security) The KGB was the intelligence and security agency in the Soviet Union from 1954 to 1991.

LISTENING POST (LP) A site at which signals received by bugs and other means of electronic audio surveillance are monitored.

MI5 (Military Intelligence, section 5) Britain's MI5 no longer has military connections. Officially called the Secret Service, it is responsible for internal security (within the UK).

MI6 (Military Intelligence, section 6) Britain's MI6 is no longer associated with the military, and is responsible for foreign intelligence. It is officially called the Secret Intelligence Service (SIS).

MICRODOT An optical reduction of a text, images, or a photographic negative to a size (usually 1 mm across or smaller) that is illegible without magnification.

MOLE An employee or officer of an intelligence service who works secretly for another intelligence service.

KGB badge

STASI (*Staatsicherheitsdienst*) East Germany's state security organization, with a section (the HVA) for conducting foreign intelligence operations. It was dissolved in 1990.

SURVEILLANCE Observation from a distance using electronic devices and other equipment, both audio and visual.

SVR (Russian abbreviation for Russian Foreign Intelligence Service) The agency that replaced the KGB's foreign intelligence-gathering section, which was disbanded in 1991.

SWEEP To check a room for bugs, often with an electronic device known as a "broom".

TELEPHONE TAPPING Also called wire tapping, telephone tapping is the monitoring of phone conversations by a third party, often by covert means.

TERRORISM Using violent acts, such as bombings, to create widespread fear amongst opponents in order to achieve a political goal.

TRANSMITTER An electronic device that generates electrical, radio, or microwave signals and sends them to a receiver.

TREASON A crime that involves a serious act of disloyalty to one's own nation.

TURN To force a spy to work against his or her original intelligence service as a double agent, usually by confronting them with evidence of their guilt and offering immunity from prosecution in exchange for cooperation.

UAV (Unmanned Aerial Vehicle) An unpiloted aircraft that is remotely controlled or directed by a preprogrammed on-board computer. UAVs are often used for military reconnaissance and attack missions, and also for espionage.

WALK-IN SPY A spy who walks in to a foreign embassy and offers to supply secrets.

WARSAW PACT The military alliance of the Soviet Union and other Communist countries in Central and Eastern Europe. It existed between 1955 and 1991, during the Cold War.

American radio transmitter and receiver used in World War II

Index

Acknowledgements

Dorling Kindersley would like to thank:
Audiotel International Limited (Keith Penny, Ray Summers, Julie Walker, Adrian Hickey); Eon Productions (Julie O'Reilly); the Imperial War Museum, London (Paul Cornish, John Bullen, Mike Hibbard); Intelligence Corps Museum, Ashford (Major R W M Shaw, Mrs Janet Carpenter); Leica UK Ltd (Peter Mulder); Lorraine Electronics Surveillance (David Benn, Simon Rosser); H Keith Melton; Next Retail Ltd (Shirley Brown, Hilary Santell); Joanne Poynor; Spycatcher (Mike Phillips); Whitbread plc (Nicholas Redman, Archivist) **Design help:** Ann Cannings, Jason Gonsalves, Sailesh Patel **Pigeon:** Rick Osman; **Pigeon parachute:** Martine Cooper; **Artwork:** John Woodcock; **Endpapers:** Iain Morris; **Index:** Marion Dent

For this edition, the publisher would also like to thank: Lisa Stock for editorial assistance; David Ekholm-JAlbum, Sunita Gahir, Susan St Louis, Lisa Stock, and Bulent Yusuf for the clipart; Sue Nicholson and Edward Kinsey for the wallchart; Hilary Bird for the index, and Stewart J Wild for proof-reading.

Picture credits:

The publisher would like to thank the following for their kind permission to reproduce their photographs:

(Key: a-above; b-below/bottom; c-centre; f-far; l-left; r-right; t-top)

akg-images: J.V. Leffdoel *Scipio Publius Cornelius* 40tl; Ullstein Bild 20bl.
Alamy Images: Ruth Grimes 17clb (voice recorder in briefcase); Jeff Morgan Technology 58b; Katharine Andriotis Photography, LLC 64-65 (background), 66-67 (background), 68-69 (background), 70-71 (background); Kolvenbach 57tl; Stocksearch 51br; Andrew Twort 10clb; Andrew H. Williams 58l.
Ancient Art & Architecture Collection: 6tl, 6bl, 6bc.
Courtesy of Apple. Apple and the Apple logo are trademarks of Apple Computer Inc., registered in the US and other countries: 15br.
Associated Press Ltd: 9tr, 29bl, 35t, 35br, 43c, 47bl, 52tr; Wire Photo 53cr.
Aviation Photographs International: 38tl.

Bildarchiv Preussischer Kulturbesitz: 25cl.
Bilderdienst Süddeutscher Verlag: 27cl.
Bridgeman Art Library: Guildhall Art Gallery, Corporation of London, Sir John Gilbert, detail from *Ego Et Rex Meus* 40cl; Private Collection, I Glasunov *Ivan The Terrible* 1989, 40bl; by courtesy of the board of Trustees of the V & A, London, Nicholas Hilliard, *Mary Queen of Scots* 28cl.
Camera Press Ltd: 35tr, 39cl; R. Artacho 55cra; S. Ferguson 42br; B. Ross 58ra.
Jean-Loup Charmet: Bibliothèque des arts décoratifs, Lucien Laforge *L'Espion*, 1916, 31tc.
Corbis: Bettmann 67c; Hulton-Deutsch Collection 66b.
DC Comics Inc.: *Spy vs Spy* is a trademark of E.C. Publications, Inc. ©1995. All rights reserved. Used with permission 42t.
Diasonic: 17tr.
DK Images: H Keith Melton Collection 70b, 70c, 70t, 71b, 71c.
Eon Productions: Keith Hamshere / United Artists (*Golden Eye*) front cover bcl, 4cb, 61tr, 61cr, 61br.
Satellite image courtesy of GeoEye. Copyright 2008. All rights reserved.: 54tl.
E.T. Archive: Biblioteca Nazionale Marciana, Venice 9tr; Musée de Versailles, Philippe de Champaigne, detail from *Cardinal Richelieu* 41cr; Staatliche Glyptothek, Munich 9tl; V & A, London 9tc.
Frank Spooner Pictures: Gamma-Liaison 9cl.
Getty Images: 66c; AFP 67t; Stuart Paton / The Image Bank 45b; Tom Stoddart Archive 67b.
Courtesy of Giggle Bug: 59tr.
Michael Holford: Musée de Bayeux / V&A, London: 8-9b.
Hulton Deutsch Collection: 8cr, 38c, 41c, 41bl, 58l, 57tc, 59br, 59l.
Imperial War Museum, London: 18cr, 23bc, 29tl, 36tr, 58br; Fougasse *Careless Talk Costs Lives* 8tr.
Courtesy of the International Spy Museum: © The House on F Street, LLC 2008. All Rights Reserved 68br; © The House on F Street, LLC 2008. All Rights Reserved. 20tl.
iStockphoto.com: 12 (camera with zoom lens); Mark Evans 55b.
The Kobal Collection: New Line 68bl.
Lockheed Martin Skunk Works®: 52-53b, 53t.
Magnum Photos Ltd: E Erwitt 43cl; S Meiselas 54bl; E Reed 17cr; Zachmann 55ca.
The Mansell Collection: 8tl.

Mary Evans Picture Library: front flap tl, 29r, 40c; J Mammen back cover tl, 12tl.
H Keith Melton: front cover br and bcr, back cover rcb, 10br, 11tl, 11tc, 11b,15br, 20cb, 23c, 27cr, 28tl, 28br, 28bl, 28tr, 30br, 36br, 37tr, 37tl, 37c, 37b, 42bl, 43tl, 43tr, 43br, 45tl, 50l, 50-51b, 51cl, 64b, 64c, 64t, 65b, 65ca, 65cb, 65t; Jerry Richards of the FBI Laboratory, Washington DC 8cl, 8c; Jack Ingram, Curator of the National Cryptologic Museum, Maryland 14cl, 14c, 27tr.
Mirror Syndication International: 27b, 50tr; Aldus Archive 24tl; Aldus Archive / Science Museum / Eileen Tweedy front cover cr, 24cl; Rijksinstituut voor Oorlogsdocumentatie 9c; National Archives, USA 26c; Public Record Office 25tl, 41 tl; © US Army 27tl.
NASA: Paul Riedel / Glenn Research Center (GRC) 5tr.
National Cryptologic Museum, Maryland: 26bl, 69c.
National Portrait Gallery, London: John De Critz, the Elder *Sir Francis Walsingham* 41 tr.
Nokia: 15bl, 16cra (mobile phone).
PA Photos: Brien Aho / AP 21tr; Cameron Davidson / AP 21bl; Betsy Gagne / AP 21br; Peter Jordan 69t; Metropolitan Police 58tr; Eckehard Schulz / AP 21tl.
Peter Newark's American Pictures: 30tl, 30bc, 31bl.
Photolibrary: 44 (main).
Popperfoto: 23tl, 31tr, 31br, 35bl, 41 br, 58cl; Reuter / S Jaffe 34br; Reuter / W McNamee 34c.
Press Association: 36bcl.
Range: Bettmann / UPI 22bl, 50c, 54br; Bettmann / UPI / Sam Schulman 50bc.
Rex Features Ltd: 7br; Action Press 38-39; Sipa-Press 39tl.
Reuters Television: front cover tl, 42cr (detail).
Ronald Grant Archive: *Stakeout* 1987, Touchstone 14bl, *Doctor No* 1962, UA / Eon 58tr, *The Ipcress File* 1965, Rank / Steven Lowndes 58tr, *The Three Musketeers* 1948, MGM 58br, *The Conversation* 1974, Paramount / Francis Ford Coppola 61bl.
Science Photo Library: Andrew Brookes / National Physical Laboratory 59cr; NRSC Ltd 52c; R. Ressmeyer, Starlight 38bc.
Science & Society Picture Library, Science Museum, London: 26tl, 66t.
Shutterstock: 57bl; Andrjuss 45c.
Spy Games Ltd, www.spy-games.com: 69b.
Topham-Picturepoint Ltd: back cover br, 10tl, 35cla, 35c, 34tl, 34tr; AP 45tc.

Werner Forman Archive: Ninja Museum Ueno, detail showing Ninja making secret signs 40bl; E Strouhal 6bl.
Jo Walton: 68t.
Worldmap-Priroda: 52tl, 52bl.

Wallchart
Alamy Images: Andrew Twort cra; **The Art Archive:** Science Museum, London / Eileen Tweedy bl; **DK Images:** H Keith Melton Collection clb, tr; RAF Museum, Hendon cl (playing card); Spycatcher cr (street scenes); **iStockphoto.com:** Philippe Devanne cr (SLR camera); **The Kobal Collection:** Danjaq / Eon / UA c; **H. K. Melton:** cl (spy rocks); **NASA:** Paul Riedel / Glenn Research Center (GRC) br.

All other images
© Dorling Kindersley
For further information see:
www.dkimages.com